A COMPLETE

SEX EDUCATION

FOR PARENTS, TEENAGERS, AND YOUNG ADULTS

A COMPLETE

SEX EDUCATION

FOR PARENTS, TEENAGERS, AND YOUNG ADULTS

JAMES LESLIE McCARY

 VAN NOSTRAND REINHOLD COMPANY

New York Cincinnati Toronto London Melbourne

Van Nostrand Reinhold Company Regional Offices:
New York Cincinnati Chicago Millbrae Dallas

Van Nostrand Reinhold Company International Offices:
London Toronto Melbourne

Copyright © 1973 by James Leslie McCary

Library of Congress Catalog Card Number: 73-8142
ISBN: 0-442-25261-7

Manufactured in the United States of America

Published by Van Nostrand Reinhold Company
450 West 33rd Street, New York, N.Y. 10001

Published simultaneously in Canada by Van Nostrand Reinhold Ltd.
15 14 13 12 11 10 9 8 7 6 5 4 3 2 1

Library of Congress Cataloging in Publication Data

McCary, James Leslie.
   A complete sex education for parents, teenagers,
and young adults.

   1. Sex instruction for youth. I. Title.
HQ35.M26   612.6'007   73-8142
ISBN 0-442-25261-7

PREFACE

During my first 20 years as a clinical psychologist and university professor I came increasingly to a recognition of the marked detriment to emotional well-being wrought by sexual ignorance and guilt. In those years, however, I limited my therapeutic efforts to relieving the distress of individual patients, young or old, who consulted me about sex-related problems. But I eventually realized that my efforts were rather like shoveling the tide, and I began addressing my energies to prevention rather than amelioration.

About 10 years ago, therefore, I introduced a semester-long course at the University of Houston that, I believed, was the first of its kind devoted solely to the subject of human sexuality. (I have subsequently learned that Alfred Kinsey once taught a very popular course in sex at the University of Indiana, but I have no details on the course work.) My own course proved to be highly popular, and enrollment grew from about 250 in the first semester to 1169 in the fifth. At that point enrollment had to be limited, because full seating capacity of the campus's largest lecture hall had been reached. Since that time enrollment has remained near maximum.

I have been both amazed and distressed by the sexual ignorance revealed by the vast majority of college students with whom I talk. This observation holds not only for students at my own university but also for those attending the various colleges and universities throughout the nation at which I lecture each year. And it is curious that the so-called good student is often abysmally ignorant about sexual matters in general and his own sex life in particular. Any knowledgeable sex educator or psychotherapist will concede that sex-related misinformation all too often causes havoc in the individual's emotional life and in his marital relationship as well.

Obviously college is not the optimum moment in time for young people to learn the basics of human sexuality, although the philosophy of "better late than never" is particularly pertinent here. Indeed, most authorities agree that the home is the place where sex education most logically should be offered. Sex information acquired in an atmosphere of love, understanding, and tenderness is far more meaningful than when it is learned in the schools or picked up in the streets (where, unfortunately, most sex education takes place). But if sex education does not take place in the home, then the schools are forced to assume that responsibility.

This book was written in an effort to fill two gaps—the lack of sex education on the part of young people and the lack of fundamental knowledge on the part of adults. Written in understandable terminology, the material is presented in an organized and teachable manner. It is designed to be read, perhaps studied, by the young person. Then the family can sit down together, if they wish, to discuss the material and clarify any lingering doubts or confusion. The subject matter is arranged to generate many in-depth discussions in which young people and their parents can (perhaps for the first time) learn to understand each other's value systems.

No author stands alone in the preparation of a manuscript. And I am no exception, for many people have stood in the shadows offering much-needed help and encouragement. The credits actually go back many years to discussions within my own family on myriad topics (including sex, of course), in which my wife LaVirle, our daughter Lesley, our son Stephen, and I freely exchanged views. To my thinking, the most significant proof of the pudding with respect to the value of this approach is the fact that both our children are now happily married and have, I think, a particularly wholesome attitude toward life and sex.

Among the many other contributors to this work are my editor Elizabeth Smith, my psychologist associate Betty Stewart, and my editorial assistant Mary Sieber. I am also indebted to John Tebbel (and to the noted psychologist Dr. Wardell Pomeroy for putting me in communication with him). A writer of obvious talent, Mr. Tebbel gave the manuscript his careful attention, smoothing the rough edges with considerable style. I am grateful to these people, and to many others who are not mentioned here.

JAMES LESLIE MC CARY, PH.D.
University of Houston

CONTENTS

A COMPLETE

SEX EDUCATION

FOR PARENTS, TEENAGERS, AND YOUNG ADULTS

What do you know about sex?

PROBABLY THE FIRST QUESTION parents should ask about a book such as this one would be about its value and benefit to their children. There has been so much controversy in recent years over the entire field of sex education that the parents' concern is quite sensible.

Without laboring the usual argued pros and cons of sex education, let me state at the outset that I am obviously a strong supporter of the notion that sex information and knowledge are of great benefit to both the young and old; otherwise I would not have written this book and would not have devoted much of my professional life to this area of human behavior. I can give many

1

arguments supported by scientific investigation as to why sex education is valuable and desirable but I know of only one argument against it—and that one argument holds for any topic or subject matter and not just sex education.

Let me discuss the negative argument first. That argument has to do with the fact that there are not enough qualified teachers of sex education and a poorly qualified teacher may cause more harm and problems than good for the students. As I said before, this holds for all subject matter. A person not qualified to teach mathematics but who is placed in the classroom for that purpose may do irreparable damage to the math background of the students. The same holds, of course, for sex education. Even if the teacher knows and can impart the factual sex information accurately, if he is not emotionally stable and has a disturbed attitude about sex or has sexual problems of his own, he can do even more damage than his mere ignorance could do.

Parents too need an abundance of accurate sex information and a freedom from anxiety about sex before they can communicate properly on this vital topic with their children. However, the very fact that you are reading this book points to the fact that you realize the importance of a sound sex education and that you want your child to have whatever benefits he can obtain from such a program. Probably the most important thing you can do with your children in this regard is to read this book thoroughly, have the children read and study it equally thoroughly, and then all of you sit down and discuss all the material in as detailed a manner as necessary. You may feel a little tense at first (perhaps more than your child will) but that will soon disappear as you have more and more discussions. From these discussions, not only will your children get accurate information, but guilt and shame and fear about sex will very likely clear up for everyone involved.

Your children are especially fortunate. Studies have shown that almost all children want their parents to give them their sex education. Unfortunately, however, fewer than half the children receive any "formal" sex teaching from their parents and the information they do receive is most often far too late and erroneous. Perhaps your children will fare better; when sex can be talked about between parent and child openly and without tension, it will be accepted for what it is, a delightful, meaningful and wholesome part of life.

At the danger of spending too much time on these introductory remarks, let me list the results of several research investigations into the value of an adequate amount of sex information.

1. Those individuals who have received an adequate sex education have a happier and longer marriage than those who have had no such education.

2. Sexual enjoyment in marriage is directly related to an adequate sex education.

3. There is a positive relationship between physical health (sexual) and sex education.

4. The incidence of premarital pregnancies decreases markedly (700%) after sex education.

5. The incidence of VD decreased by one half after a sex education program was introduced into a high school. The incidence rose to its previous high level when the sex education program was removed from the school.

6. The incidence of sexual inadequacies such as impotency, premature ejaculation, orgasmic difficulties, vaginismus, etc., is markedly less among people who have received adequate sex education.

7. Sexual maladjustment in marriages (estimated at 50% to 60%) is found much less among couples who have had an adequate sex education than among those who have not.

8. The incidence of premarital sexual intercourse decreases in direct proportion to the amount and accuracy of sex information girls receive.

9. The more accurate sex information parents give their children the less likely those children are ever to read or be interested in pornographic and obscene material.

10. Emotional instability, repression and anxiety in all aspects and areas of life—including, but not only, sex—

are more likely to be found among those individuals with low sex information or poor sex education than among those persons with an adequate sex education.

If I were a teenager picking up this book, the first question I think I'd have would not be about sex at all. It would be about the author, this man who intends to tell me what he thinks I should know about human sexuality. Does he know what he's talking about? Why does he think he can teach me anything about sex, anything I can't get from my friends and my own experience? Is he going to give me the same old doubletalk I get from other adults? Does he understand how young people are living now?

These are a few of the questions I'd ask. I believe they deserve an honest answer, so before I say anything about sex, let me tell you something about who I am and why I came to write this book.

I was born and brought up in a small Texas town, where I managed to learn all the wrong things about sex. My schoolroom was behind the barn door, and my teachers were friends who had more experience than I did. Actually, as I found out later, they were just as ignorant and confused about sex as I was, but that didn't prevent them from passing out information that seemed impressive but proved to be dangerous, as I discovered later.

It took me a long time to realize that my friends really felt inadequate in sexual matters. In fact, they felt threatened by sex and by their own ignorance of it, and in teaching me and other willing learners they were simply trying to impress us in order to feel important themselves. People who feel inadequate often preach loudly on subjects they don't know much about.

I estimate the sex information I got while I was growing up was about 80 percent completely wrong, and the other 20 percent at least partly incorrect. The whole thing was colored by fear, guilt, shame, much snickering and too much mystery. Long after I first needed it, I got some better education from my father and my older brother, but even with them, the information they gave me reflected their own lack of factual information and their confusion about human sexuality. The books about sex I managed to obtain and read were not much better. Most of them were inadequate in several different ways—vague, moralistic and quite often plain wrong as they set forth the writers' one-sided views.

Eventually, in college, I learned where to get accurate information, and afterward I spent more than twenty-five years as a psychotherapist and marriage counselor, as well as being a teacher, counselor and friend of college students. In carrying on these two careers, I have had a great deal of opportunity to see how damaging the lack of a sound sex education can be to the mental health of both young and old, and how great a threat it can be to the success of a marriage—or, for that matter, to the success of any kind of sex relationship between two people. It has become clear to me that a sound and unemotional presentation of sex information can do a great deal to help people toward psychological good health and happiness, whether they are married or not. From the thousands of sexual problems I have confronted in my patients over the past quarter-century and the efforts I have made to find answers that will solve them has come this book, which I hope will provide just such information and produce that happy result.

I have tried to keep moral judgments out of what follows in this volume, at least those of the conventional kind which are usually attached to efforts at sex education. But that doesn't mean I have no moral standpoint. My belief is that in the entire area of human relationships, whether they involve individuals or nations, we can only grow and develop if these relationships have their roots in fundamental principles of honesty, decency and fair play. These are principles embodied in Judeo-Christian teachings, but they are also fundamental in all the world's religions.

There is another conviction I have about this matter. I believe that acts have consequences, that causes are followed by effects, and so people who stray too far or too often from these basic principles are going to suffer in one way or another, either from the disapproval of the society in which they happen to live, or from their own consciences. Consequently, in talking about sex, we are not discussing purely physical actions, but the ethical implications of the actions we take, and the necessity to think about them before we do something. There may be room for argument about some ethical distinctions, but there is one certain guide in all human behavior, sexual or otherwise, which seems to me unarguable. "Do unto others as you would have them do unto you," says the Bible, although not in those exact words. People who follow that principle don't take advantage of other people, and they don't damage their own self-respect.

Having introduced myself and my attitudes, and assuming you accept both, I'll now get back to the question that heads this chapter, "What do you know about sex?"

Only boasters and pretenders would answer, "I know everything about it," or reply, "All I need to know." There are few people who could make either of these statements honestly, and that includes most adults. If I could talk to every reader of this book and ask him that question, I feel sure that everyone who gave me a frank answer would admit that he didn't know everything he wanted to know about sex, and that what he did know had not been learned soon enough. It is safe to say, too, that most teenagers would report that most of what they got from adults was embarrassment, obvious ignorance, avoidance of the subject, or even anger when the subject was mentioned.

But you *do* have the right to know. The proper use of sex, free from shame or guilt, brings a joy, a fulfillment, an intimacy that is the most special of all human experiences. Yet it is a shame of our educational system that the subject of sex is by-passed, mistaught, or studied only on the biological level. On that level, it is easy enough to deal with sex in a straightforward manner, although this was not always so. But when it comes to the emotional and ethical aspects, feelings of embarrassment have an unfortunate way of creeping into sex education. Embarrassment seems to make people laugh, giggle, or joke about it. This tells the experienced observer that they are poorly educated about sex, fearful of it, or simply immature. Not that we need to approach sex always in a solemn, sober manner. Fun and laughter are part of it too, rising from acceptance of its simple joyousness.

Parents have to accept a large part of the responsibility for teenagers' ignorance and confusion about sex. A recent survey disclosed that the one point on which a group of high school honor students were most critical of their parents was their failure to discuss human sexuality with them. Two-thirds reported that their parents had told them nothing, and the others had been given only superficial information, much of it inaccurate. Another sampling of a hundred teenage boys and another hundred girls showed that in a list of thirty topics all the students marked sex as the most difficult one to discuss with their parents.

I don't think things have changed much in this respect from my own boyhood—a really startling idea, when we think of how vastly different the sexual climate in America is today. Young people still get most of their information about sex as they grow up from their friends, usually in conversation, often in the form of bad jokes, full of misinformation. Secondarily (and it is a bad second) they learn from their parents. Very little comes from schools and other institutions. Most of those who do get accurate information about their sexuality learn too late to help them through the early and difficult stages of sexual development and adjustment in adolescence.

All this accounts for the common story, perpetuated by adults, about the young girl or boy who is sat down by his parents for a formal talk about the "facts of life," as the cliché goes, and it turns out that the son or daughter already knows as much or more than his parents, although what both sides know may be some distance from the truth.

Surveys have shown us how badly parents fail here. In one, two-thirds of the boys questioned reported they already knew about sexual intercourse from other sources before their parents got around to discussing it with them for the first time. In another study, about 70 percent of the women questioned reported they had been led to believe, chiefly by their mothers, that sex is dirty. Girls seem to be especially vulnerable. One study cited "early sex education from parents" as the *only* factor in women's backgrounds and early histories that was actually related to the adequacy of their sexual response as adults.

We shouldn't blame the parents too harshly, though. Teenagers are inclined to do that, but they ought to remember that the parents themselves are often filled with shame and guilt about sex. They are painfully uncertain as to what they understand and really believe about sexuality and what constitutes acceptable sexual behavior. Not only are they afraid or ashamed to admit their confusion over the true meaning of sex, but they often have very little accurate information on the subject to give their children. And the less information a person has, the more difficult it is for him to talk about sexual matters.

Unfortunately, the unhealthy feelings about sex that some parents have can cause their children to acquire, directly or indirectly, the same disturbed attitudes, with the result that they run the risk of going through life as a kind of emotional cripple where sex is concerned.

Ignorance about sex is doubly a shame these days because we know so much more about it than we used to. Before Dr. Kinsey began his famous research into human sexual behavior, about 1941, there had been only nineteen scientific studies of sex in this country since the beginning of the century, and few of these were of much significance. Since then, we have had Kinsey's landmark books about men, in 1948, and women, in 1953, and a small but dedicated body of scientists in recent years has been studying human sexuality with the same objectivity scientific researchers have long used in other fields. Americans are so uptight about sex, however, that the work of these researchers has met with suspicion, prejudice and downright hostility on the part of a large section of the general public, and even from some of their fellow scientists.

Physicians, psychologists and sociologists have brought some of this opposition on themselves. Sometimes they have added to the confusion about sex because their approaches to the subject have been too much conditioned by their individual attitudes, beliefs and personal problems.

You, as teenagers, might reasonably ask how you can be expected to acquire healthy feelings about sex when the adult society is unable to agree on sexual matters, and when parents, teachers and scientists too often lack the proper training or objectivity to teach you properly. It's a good question. The answer is that adults are going to have to work to correct their own confused sexual attitudes, and re-educate themselves about sex. When young people are taught early enough and in sufficient detail about sex, the vicious cycle of handing down ignorance from one generation to another will be broken.

Since parents are usually too uninformed and too embarrassed to do the job, and since religious organizations are so often emotional, prejudiced and erroneous in their understanding of the facts, the schools appear to be the best place to present sex education material without guilt, shame and fear.

Teachers are not likely to insist that healthy males and females should avoid or shut off all expression of their sexual needs and drives, as home and church so often do. This is unrealistic, to say the least. Every culture and subculture permit various means of expressing sexuality, and it is well known that sexual needs will find expression one way or another. By not permitting healthy expressions of the sexual impulse, we only encourage its expression in the form of mental illnesses, personality difficulties, guilt, feelings of inadequacy, and true sexual abnormalities. A physician wrote in the last part of the nineteenth century that he believed not one bride in a hundred expected ever to get any sexual gratification. He didn't say so, but no doubt his office was filled with ailing ladies whose sexuality found expression in imaginary illnesses—even as they do today.

Psychologists call the diversion of feelings from one channel to another, "displacement." People who are unable or unwilling to express their sexual needs directly, "displace" this expression into some other kind of behavior. For example, those who are disturbed by the thought of sexual relationships outside of marriage express an unconscious interest in such acts, or perhaps a desire for them, by showing an excessive interest in those activities. These are the people who express horror or contempt or amusement over the sexual behavior of actors and actresses, yet read every detail about what they do, and fill the theaters where they perform. They satisfy their own desires by identifying with these personalities, and at the same time avoid feelings of guilt by pointing an accusing finger at them.

Similarly, tensions generated by rigid controls on personal sexual behavior are drained off by joking and laughter about sex, or talking about it in a vulgar way, or ridiculing the sexual behavior of others. Control of, and proper expression of, sexual needs, according to time and place, are necessary, but to set up unrealistic barriers is an invitation to trouble.

If anyone doubts that people in general, not just teenagers, don't know as much as they say they do about sex, we need only to look around and see how our guilt, shame and unreasonable attitudes about sex are expressed, at both ends of the scale. Nudity is used on the covers of paperback books and magazines to sell everything from murder mysteries to essays on seal hunting among the Eskimos. Women in various states of undress decorate the covers of the most popular magazines, some of which are devoted to sex in one way or another. Women with seductive voices and sexy figures sell everything from shoe polish to salad dressing in advertisements, particularly on television. Film advertising is often directed frankly to sexual interest.

While all this is going on, a large number of people, including organized laymen and politicians who want votes, spend a great deal of time trying to suppress all these misdirected methods of handling the sexual drive. Sometimes their activities are absurd. In Birmingham, England, a department store aroused a storm of protest with a window full of mannequins clad in sexy lingerie. The only way the owner could deal with the protest was to put wedding rings on the fingers of the wax models. In America, the Society for the Prevention of Indecency to Naked Animals started out as a joke, the members arguing solemnly that children should be protected from the sight of naked animals, particularly cattle, dogs and cats, by putting clothes on them if they were to appear in public or before children. Astonishingly, so many indignant people who failed to get the joke jumped on the bandwagon that the organization became at least semi-legitimate.

People are equally ambivalent about sex in movies. As everyone knows, the sexier a film is today the better it does at the boxoffice, and hardcore pornography itself is a boxoffice success. People cover their guilt about all this by sanctioning drives to eliminate or limit sexy pictures, and by setting up artificial age distinctions which say that a motion picture may harm a teenager the day before he is seventeen but not the day after. To compound this confusion, the age of innocence is set at different figures according to states or cities.

Parents are wrong if they believe children will avoid sex if they don't know about it. Nothing could be farther from the truth, and it is dangerous to think so. For example, parents often refuse to give their children any information about contraception or venereal disease. For information they substitute moralistic warnings about the shame and danger of illegitimate pregnancy and VD in the mistaken belief that this will keep their teenagers from having sexual intercourse before they are married. But long before the Pill and modern methods of dealing with VD, only 44 percent of the married women interviewed by Kinsey listed "fear of pregnancy" as having discouraged them from engaging in sexual intercourse, and only 15 percent listed "fear of venereal disease." We can only guess at what the figures would be today, since no massive studies like Kinsey's have been made since his death in 1956, but a recent survey of unmarried pregnant girls showed that they had been given little or no sex education either at home or school; their mothers either lacked proper knowledge of sex or were unable or unwilling to give proper instruction to their daughters.

If I seem to be talking more about parents here in these opening pages than about teenagers, it is simply because I want the teenagers to see that they are not alone in their ignorance and anxieties, and that the problem of sex education is a larger one than they may have thought. We need more understanding of the whole thing, rather than arguments about details.

We need it especially because of what has become a common problem these days, premarital pregnancy. No matter how liberated the teenager involved may be, or how understanding the parents (and not many are), it is a situation which still causes great distress to everyone involved. And when such a pregnancy is permitted to push a teenage couple into a marriage they are not likely to be ready for, emotionally, physically or financially, there is every reason for gloom. Educations are halted, resentments build up, girls and boys alike may feel trapped, careers are handicapped. Not many of these marriages succeed with such handicaps at the start. Abortion is the only alternative, and while the Supreme Court has now made that medically legal and feasible in every state of the union, it is not an experience that many would contemplate with joy or anticipation.

With this state of affairs readily acknowledged by both teenagers and their parents, it is hard to understand why opinion in this country is still so strongly divided about whether to give contraceptive information to unmarried people. It ought to be an important part of any course in sex education, and where no such course exists, it should be given by any means possible—especially when we know that one in six brides is pregnant when she marries, with the highest percentage among teenagers. Those who console themselves with the idea that religious principles will keep the young from having premarital sex should know that while this may be true in some cases, it is certainly not true in others; unwanted pregnancies also occur among the religiously devout.

Any therapist could talk endlessly about the need for young people to have sex information of all kinds. He could quote the World Health Organization's statement that ignorance and not knowledge of sexual matters is the cause of "sexual misadventure." Psychotherapists and marriage counselors can only say "amen" to that.

I urge teenagers to understand that no matter what they think they know about sex, the chances are they need a great deal more education if they are going to have satisfactory personal relationships as adults. Understanding why parents are so often inadequate teachers alleviates tension in the family, but it is no substitute for getting the information elsewhere.

It will be no news to teenagers that the adults in their lives are mostly counting on guilt to control their sexual behavior, and all too often the adults succeed in ways that were not intended. It is controlled, all right, even when it takes place after the marriage vows are spoken, and the bride and groom begin to try to break out of the guilty pattern which says that sex is dirty, that sex equals sin. No wonder that guilt, pain, frigidity, impotency and premature ejaculation are part of the honeymoon. If people feel guilty about sex and are made to think there is something wrong with it before marriage, it will not be changed into something beautiful and happy by the words of the marriage ceremony.

One thing about sex education that is better understood by parents than by teenagers, although the former may not express it, is that such education begins long before nursery school. It begins, really, with the first close mother-infant contact after birth. The way in which mothers and fathers love, play with, and even hold the baby; the soothing or harsh sound of parents' voices, which are associated either with love or rejection and hostility; the feel of the parents' skin and the smell of their bodies—all these are important in the development of children's sexual attitudes and conduct. A child's sex education begins in the earliest days of his life. It is education even when parents avoid discussing sex, because the child senses such attitudes as readily as he does the others.

Attitudes are important. How can anyone judge intelligently the value of a particular moral code, and decide for himself the effects of various kinds of sexual behavior on himself, his partner and society without information on which to base his decisions? True, he can go by instinct or on the basis of what he *does* know, however little it may be, but that is not much help in making good decisions.

Teenagers, more than parents, realize that there are individual differences in learning anything, and sex education is no different. "I'm not ready," a girl may say, or a boy will protest, "I don't want to." Since they have not yet been hammered into adult patterns of conformity, teenagers are by and large rather tolerant about trying to make others accept personal beliefs. To some extent, at least, they have respect for the rights of other teenagers, including an acceptance of individual tastes and pleasures. "Do your own thing," we say now. No one has the moral right to force his ethical views on his neighbors, and he ought not to have the legal right to do so.

But there is one thing we should all agree on, even though we don't, and that is the necessity for a sound sex education for everyone. Society will never achieve sexual stability without it. We need education, not indoctrination; facts, not fallacies; objectivity, not subjectivity; democracy, not autocracy.

If you, as a teenager, think you know something about sex, ask yourself honestly if you have a thorough understanding of these fundamentals:

1. Do you understand thoroughly the physiological structure of the male and female reproductive systems?

2. Do you know the relationship between sexuality and your role in society?

3. Do you understand the various attitudes toward sex and how they relate to sexual behavior?

4. Do you really understand the nature of the sex drive and its relationship to love and marriage?

That much for starters. And not to mention such subjects as masturbation, contraception, abortion, pregnancy, homosexuality, frigidity, impotence and other differences in sexual behavior. Do you *really* know all you think you know about sexual intercourse? And so on through a long list which this book will cover.

I hope to provide you with a giant step toward real sex education with this book. But with or without it, you should not feel inadequate if you are willing to admit you don't know enough and want to learn more. Look for professional help wherever you can get it—from other books, from school, from anyone qualified to give it. Your success in becoming informed will have a direct effect on all your relationships and will go a long way toward making your adult life happier.

2

Bodies: The marvelous machines

KNOWLEDGE ABOUT SEX begins with how we are put together—what people commonly call their plumbing, meaning their reproductive organs. Important as this knowledge is, it is not the most fascinating material you're going to read here. The terms can be confusing, too. Following the diagrams will help, and it is worth paying attention because it is ignorance of these basic facts, or misunderstandings about them, which cause so much anxiety among teenagers. Learning how the reproductive system works is the beginning of wisdom, and more than a superficial knowledge is needed.

Let's begin with the male sexual apparatus. The seat of reproduction is in the *testicles*,

15

also called *testes,* the male sex glands. It is these organs which produce the male germ cells, the sperm. Testes develop in pairs in the body cavity and descend until they hang between the legs in a bag called the *scrotum,* a loose pouch of skin.

These testicles are egg-shaped bodies. They vary in size, although in adults they usually measure about an inch by an inch-and-a-half. The temperature of the scrotum is usually slightly lower than that of the body itself; that is necessary for the production of sperm. Testicles are supported by muscles and tissues which contract when the outside temperature is low, pulling them close to the warmer body and relaxing when the temperature is high, lowering them away from the body. Boys often notice that their testicles—or "balls," in the common language—draw closer to the body not only in cold weather but in a cold shower, and in some emotional circumstances involving fear and tension.

Inside each testicle are several hundred small compartments, each containing several tiny coiled tubes in which sperm are produced. The spaces between these tubes are filled with cells that produce male hormones, and the walls of the tubes are lined with the tissue that produces sperm in a continuing process of manufacture called *spermatogenesis.*

Sperm are the organisms that carry the male's contribution to the reproductive process. Their active production usually begins in a boy when he is about 11 years old, although the age varies considerably from boy to boy. The inner lining of the sperm-producing tubes, where the manufacture of sperm begins, contains the basic sperm cells. Through a process of cell division, each of the basic sperm cells divides into two cells, one of which remains in the inner lining of the tubule, ready to split again. This assures that there will always be basic cells ready for future division. It can thus be seen that it is impossible for a male to "use up" his supply of sperm, as is thought by some. The other new cell moves inward toward the central opening of the tube. As it does so, it divides into two smaller cells.

At this point the paired chromosomes, including the XY pair, also divide in such a way that half go to one of these new cells and half to the other. Consequently one new cell gets

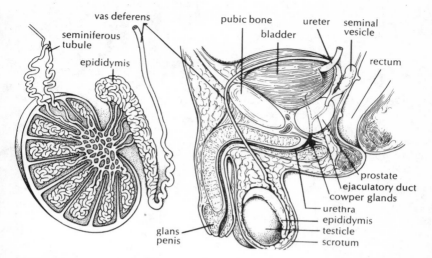

vas deferens

seminiferous tubule

epididymis

pubic bone

bladder

ureter

seminal vesicle

rectum

prostate
ejaculatory duct
cowper glands
urethra
epididymis
testicle
scrotum

glans penis

Enlargement of cross section of a testicle.

Cross section of the male pelvic region showing the reproductive system.

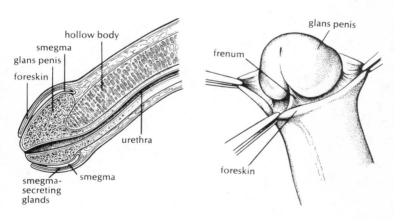

hollow body

smegma
glans penis
foreskin

urethra

smegma-
secreting
glands

smegma

glans penis

frenum

foreskin

Cross section of penis showing collection of smegma. Hollow body is filled with spongy erectile tissue. When the spongy tissue fills with blood the penis becomes erect.

Foreskin pulled back to show glans penis.

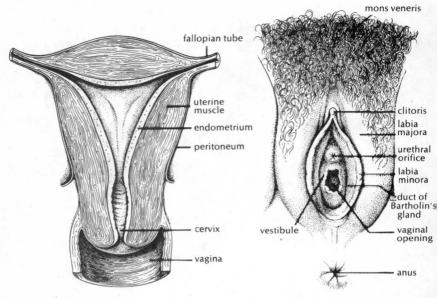

Cross section of the uterus showing the three layers of the uterine wall.

The external female genitalia.

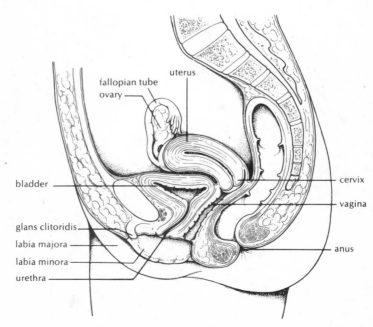

Cross section of the female pelvic region showing the internal female sex organs.

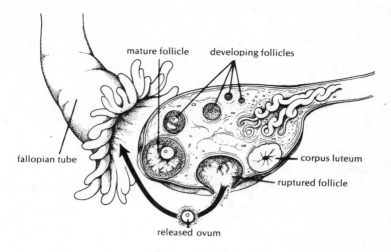

Cross section of an ovary. Note developing follicles and corpus luteum.

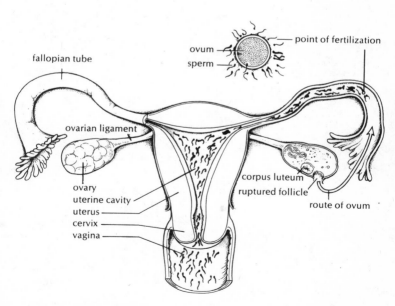

Cross section of the female reproductive system showing route of discharged mature ovum from ovary. Note sperm fertilizing mature ovum in fallopian tube.

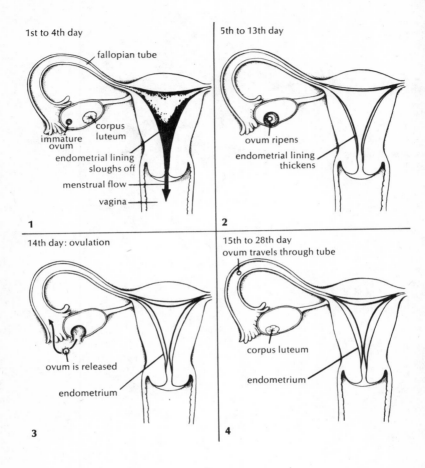

1st to 4th day

fallopian tube

corpus
luteum

immature
ovum

endometrial lining
sloughs off

menstrual flow

vagina

1

5th to 13th day

ovum ripens

endometrial lining
thickens

2

14th day: ovulation

ovum is released

endometrium

3

15th to 28th day
ovum travels through tube

corpus luteum

endometrium

4

1. Menstruation phase. If ovum is not fertilized, the endometrium breaks down and is discharged as menstrual bleeding. 2. Postmenstruation phase. Menstrual flow has stopped and the uterine lining thickens. 3. Ovulation phase. The Graafian follicle, housing the mature ovum, ruptures. The ovum is released and travels through the fallopian tube. 4. Premenstruation phase. The corpus luteum develops and produces progesterone. The uterine lining continues to thicken.

the X, or female-producing, chromosome and the other gets the Y, or male-producing, chromosome. So the X- and Y-bearing sperm are always produced in equal numbers.

In the next step of sperm development, the two secondary sperm split, this time forming the *spermatids,* which will develop into mature sperm, also called *spermatozoa.* This whole process, from beginning to end, is called spermatogenesis, the making of sperm, and in the healthy adult male it takes about ten days and goes on all the time, day and night.

Are you still with me? All right, then, we've produced the sperm and they are ready to go on the first stage of their journey. Follow your diagram now. The sperm move from the epididymis into another small tube, about 18 inches long, called the *vas deferens,* or sometimes the *vas* or *ductus deferens.* It is actually a continuation of the epididymis. The vas leads from the testicle up into the body cavity and to the top of the prostate gland. There it is joined by the *seminal vesicle,* a bulb-shaped structure about 4½ inches long when it is stretched. The seminal vesicle produces a secretion that helps the prostatic fluid to activate and transport the sperm, and it is also believed to serve as a storage compartment for some of the sperm.

Each of the two vas deferens joins the *ejaculatory duct,* which passes through the prostate gland and into the *urethra,* the urinary tube leading from the bladder out through the penis.

Now the sperm gets an added ingredient from the *prostate,* a firm, partly muscular, partly glandular body about the size of a walnut. It is located immediately below the bladder and surrounds its neck and the upper part of the urethra. The prostate has two main functions. One is to produce the greater portion of the *ejaculatory fluid,* and this, when mixed with the sperm, forms the *semen,* the fluid that is discharged from the penis. You may think it is superfluous to say so, but it is surprising how many young boys do not know that the penis, which they commonly call the "cock," is the organ that is inserted in the woman's vagina during sexual intercourse, and out of it comes the semen, known as ejaculation, which carries all the male's contribution to the making of a baby when it unites with the female egg. This sudden discharge of semen, accompanied by highly pleasurable sensations, is the orgasm, the peak of sexual enjoyment in the male.

The prostate has another function as well. It stores the sperm, allowing it to mix with the ejaculatory fluid. When ejaculation occurs, the prostate forces the semen through the ejaculatory ducts by means of sudden muscular contractions, and it goes through these ducts into the urethra and out of the penis in a squirting fashion. Semen, also known as seminal fluid, is a milky-looking, highly alkaline liquid containing many substances, including protein, calcium, citric acid, cholesterol, various enzymes and other acids.

Just below the prostate, on each side of the urethra, are two pea-sized bodies, *Cowper's glands*. During sexual excitation, these glands secrete a few drops of an alkaline fluid called *precoital fluid,* which lubricates the male's urethra. This fluid usually appears at the tip of the penis during sexual excitement before ejaculation occurs. In most cases, the precoital fluid does not contain any sperm, but recent studies have shown that it does in about 25 percent of cases.

This is worth remembering for boys who have already tried intercourse, and think they are preventing a girl from getting pregnant by withdrawing before they ejaculate. "Just putting it in," as they call it, can be very risky if no other precautions are taken.

The base of the penis is situated just below Cowper's glands. In adult men, the length of the average penis is from 3 to 4 inches in its limp, or flaccid, state, and it is about 1 inch in diameter. When the penis is hard or in a state of erection, also called tumescence, the average adult penis is 5½ to 6½ inches long and about 1½ inches in diameter. Penis measurements, both limp and erect, vary considerably from man to man.

Boys often worry unnecessarily about the size of their penises. There is no reason at all to worry. Length of the penis has nothing to do with the enjoyment of sex. Further, there is little relationship between the size of a penis when it is limp and when it is erect, nor is there as much relationship between the size of the penis and general body size as there is between the size of other organs and body size. One man may have a penis

2 inches long, and another's may be 10 inches, but one is as capable of having pleasurable sexual intercourse as the other.

Don't worry, consequently, if you do not have a large penis. In spite of all the stories you may hear, the size of your sex organ has little or nothing to do with the pleasure and satisfaction either you or a partner will have from sexual intercourse. Even if this were not true, there is nothing anyone can do to alter the size of a penis. Heredity determines its size. Only in rare cases where some kind of hormonal imbalance has occurred and impaired the growth of the sex organs can medical treatment increase size and functional ability.

The penis is the most familiar part of a boy's body and is probably the one he knows least about. Its shaft, or body, is made up of three cylindrical bodies composed of spongy tissue. During sexual excitement, the arteries and veins function so that blood flows into the spongy tissue and becomes trapped there, causing the penis to become hard and erect. After orgasm and ejaculation have occurred (or if all sexual excitement is stopped for a while), the arteries and veins reverse their function so that less blood flows into the penis than drains off from it. That causes the penis to return to its normal limp state shortly after the sex act.

At the end of the penis is the *glans,* a smooth, conelike head. It is by far the most sexually sensitive part of a man's body. The ridge of the glans and the bit of thin loose tissue on the underside of the glans known as the *frenum* are especially sensitive to sexual stimulation.

In its original state, the penis has a loose flap of unattached skin extending from the body of the penis to cover the glans, so loose it can be pulled back to allow the penis to expand to full erection. This is known as the *foreskin,* or *prepuce.* It is usually cut away these days, either for religious reasons, as in the Jewish faith, or because many doctors regard it as routine surgical procedure at birth. For whatever reason, this process is called *circumcision.*

While there are arguments for and against circumcision, aside from religious ritual, many doctors advise it on the ground that it may prevent annoying small difficulties. One is that if the foreskin is not circumcised, and if a man doesn't pull it back and cleanse the area thoroughly, a smelly cheese-like substance called smegma may accumulate, composed of an oily secretion and dead cells that have been secreted and shed from the glans. In other cases, the foreskin may be so tight over the glans that it is difficult to pull it back to clean the area under it. If it is that tight, it may also make erection painful. Consequently circumcision is routine, although not really essential.

A penis cannot penetrate the vagina unless it is erect. Erection can be brought about in a variety of ways. Some of them are physical, like touching or massaging the penis or surrounding areas. Others are psychological, like kissing or even the sight of a girl who is liked or loved. Or it may be sexual thoughts arising from dreams, or reading books or seeing erotic films. The odor of perfume can do it. At other times the cause may be physiological, like a heavy concentration of sex hormones in the bloodstream, and sexual tensions caused by full ejaculatory ducts.

If enough physical or psychological stimulation is applied long enough, a man will get and maintain an erection. On the other hand, there are many factors that will prevent an erection from occurring, or cause the penis to collapse before ejaculation. They may be physical, as when there is such strong stimulation of the penis that actual pain may be the result; or they can be psychological, as in such negative influences as fear, anxiety, anger or shame.

In ordinary circumstances, erection occurs before ejaculation. The same stimulations that bring about and maintain an erection also build up impulses in the ejaculatory center of the lower spinal cord to a point where there is a sudden triggering of the process. But ejaculation and orgasm can also take place without any physical or conscious psychological stimulation. The common example is the *nocturnal emission,* more familiarly known as a "wet dream." This is the result of erotic dreams, and may occur after a long period in which there has been no sexual release, or shortly after such a release.

Boys sometimes play a game in which they masturbate to see which one can shoot out semen the farthest when they ejaculate. The winners may imagine they are more masculine, but the fact is that the strength of ejaculatory force varies considerably from male to male, and has no relationship to masculinity. Some men ejaculate with such force that the discharged semen may spurt three feet or more beyond the tip of the penis, while for others the semen spurts only a few inches or simply oozes from the penis. Several factors influence the strength of ejaculation, like general health, age, degree of sexual excitation and the condition of the prostate.

Let's turn now to the female sexual system, which consists internally of the ovaries, the uterine or Fallopian tubes, the uterus or womb, and the vagina.

Girls have sex glands, or gonads, too, called *ovaries*. They serve the same purpose for females that testicles do for men, and they also develop in pairs. Unlike the testicles, however, they are situated in the abdominal cavity. Out of the ovaries comes the female's contribution to the reproductive process, the eggs, known as ova—or ovum, if you're talking about only one egg. Ovaries also manufacture certain hormones which figure in a woman's sex drive and her ability to reproduce. Although we cannot see the ovaries, they are pinkish-gray organs roughly the size, shape and weight of an unshelled almond. They are placed one on each side of the uterus.

Inside the ovary of an adult woman are a number of tiny round cavities, or sacs, called *follicles*. Each of these contains an ovum at some stage of development. If it were possible to examine all these follicles separately, it would be plain that some have not begun growing while others have started the maturing process and are approaching the time when a fully developed ovum will break through the follicle wall and be discharged from the ovary.

One follicle, called the *Graafian follicle*, becomes fully mature each month. At maturity it is quite large, often occupying as much as one-fourth of the entire volume of the ovary. This human ovum, housed in the follicle, is one of the largest eggs produced by mammals—but it is smaller than the period at the end of this sentence.

It may be hard to believe, but in each ovary of a newborn girl there are about 200,000 to 400,000 follicles, each housing an undeveloped egg. This number, however, may decrease to as little as 10,000 by the time puberty arrives. As I've said, one follicle and one ovum develop into maturity every month in the physically mature female. Since the average woman is capable of bearing children for about 35 years, and ovulates (that is, discharges an egg) thirteen times a year, a little quick arithmetic tells us that only 400 or 500 ova ever reach maturity and are discharged from the ovary. The remaining follicles and their undeveloped ova simply waste away.

This process, the development of a human ovum, is known as *oogenesis*. Although the process takes longer, it is a little like spermatogenesis, the manufacture of sperm in the male which I described a little earlier.

The basic cell of the ovum is called the *oogonium,* and is housed in one of the ovarian follicles. In its second stage of development it becomes somewhat larger and then it is called the *primary oocyte.* Just before ovulation, this primary oocyte divides into two new cells in such a way that 23 of its 46 chromosomes go into each. One of these two cells does not function and eventually wastes away. The other cell, a larger one, is called the *secondary oocyte.* This cell also divides into two cells, and again the smaller cell does not function while the larger one becomes a fully developed ovum capable of being fertilized.

The ovaries are connected to the uterus by means of the two *Fallopian tubes.* These tubes, measuring about 4 inches in length, extend from each side of the upper portion of the uterus, and then broaden to cup over the ovaries slightly at the point where they are attached.

Once the ovarian follicle has ruptured and the ovum escapes from it, the egg enters the Fallopian tube on the same side of the body, although sometimes there are exceptions. If fertilization is to take place, the sperm meets and penetrates the ovum in the Fallopian tube. That happens when the male, inserting his penis in the female's vagina, shoots out his seminal fluid during orgasm, and the released sperm start swimming their way toward the location of the egg. If sperm and egg meet and fertilization takes place, the fertilized egg moves on into the uterus and implants itself in the wall there. If it is not fertilized, the egg wastes away in the Fallopian tube.

Once the ovum is discharged from the ovary, the lining of the empty follicle grows inward and the vacated space is filled with a yellow body called the *corpus luteum,* which produces the hormone called progesterone. If the recently discharged egg becomes fertilized, the hormone prevents further ovulation during the pregnancy. Progesterone also helps to implant and maintain the fertilized egg. When the ovum is not fertilized, the corpus luteum shrinks away and no more progesterone is produced until the next ovum is discharged.

Scientists believe that ovulation usually occurs from each ovary in alternate months, but in some cases one ovary may actually discharge several times in succession. Ordinarily a single egg is released at the time of ovulation, but two or more ova from one or more follicles may be discharged—and that's how the births of nonidentical twins come about.

Now that the fertilized egg has been implanted in the uterus wall and begun to grow, a further remarkable development takes place. Remarkable because the womb is a hollow, thick-walled muscular organ shaped a little like a pear, measuring at the top (in mature women) about 2 by 2½ inches, and narrowing to a diameter of about 1 inch at the *cervix* at the lower end, where it opens into the vagina. The entire length of the uterus is only about 3 inches, situated slightly below and between the Fallopian tubes, as though it were hung from them like a garment from a clothesline. It is located between the bladder and the rectum.

Yet in this small space the baby grows until it is ready to be delivered. To understand how that is possible, we have to examine the womb to see the way it's put together. It is divided into two parts by a slight narrowing near the center. The larger part is above the smaller part, the cervix. The walls of the womb, which are particularly thick at the top, are made up of three layers. Elastic fibrous tissue composes the outer layer. Bundles and layers of very strong smooth muscles make up the middle layer, and this constitutes most of the uterine wall. The inner layer, known as the *endometrium,* consists of tissue that thickens as the uterus prepares for the fertilized ovum to plant itself there. If no pregnancy occurs, part of this inner tissue will be cast off at the time of menstruation.

Muscle fibers spiral through the uterine walls, in both clockwise and counterclockwise directions, like a woven basket. This interweaving of muscles allows the uterus to stretch and expand to large proportions during pregnancy, and that is what you see when you observe a pregnant woman with her belly very much blown up. It is the amazing, muscular, flexible uterus, expanding to take care of the growing baby. When it is time for the child to be born, these muscles are also able to exert tremendous downward pressure so that the baby can be expelled from the womb.

In its normal state, the cavity or hollow of the uterus is about 2½ inches long, a flattened space little more than a slit. The cavity narrows to an opening smaller than a soda straw at the cervix. About a half inch of the cervix extends into the vagina, permitting the passage of the sperm on its way to a possible meeting with an ovum in the Fallopian tube.

The *vagina* is a muscular tube extending from just behind the cervix to an external opening in the vulva, that is, the female sex organs visible outside. In its normal state, the vagina is about 3½ inches long. When a girl is standing up, it is in approximately a vertical position, roughly at right angles to the uterus. Picture the vagina as a kind of sheath which receives the penis during intercourse.

In their normal state, the walls of the vagina touch each other. The inner surface has large folds in it, however, which make it look wrinkled but allow it to expand. Not only does the vagina receive the penis in intercourse, but it is the passageway through which a baby travels when it is born, so the degree of expansion it is capable of is not hard to imagine. To make it easier for the penis to penetrate, the walls of the vagina have a kind of sweating mechanism which makes them wet, thereby providing lubrication during sexual excitement. To those who think there is nothing new to be learned about sex, I can point out that this mechanism has only recently been discovered. I might add, too, that the vagina has still another function: it provides the passageway for the menstrual fluid to flow out.

A popular belief among adolescents, and a good many adults as well, is that women ejaculate, like men. That idea tems from the "sweating" process that goes on in the vaginal walls. As sexual excitement builds up and continues, little eads of "sweat" appear on these walls. Sometimes the muscles surrounding the vagina contract suddenly, bringing the walls together so that they force the fluid out of the vagina o forcefully that in some cases it appears to spurt. Combined with the muscular contractions of the vagina just before and during orgasm, the whole process may convince the ordinary observer that he is seeing something more or less like the male's ejaculation, when actually it is quite a different phenomenon. Erotic literature from many different countries has helped to perpetuate this myth.

Another part of female anatomy surrounded by a considerable amount of myth is the *hymen,* commonly known as the *maidenhead.* We can see readily enough how it came to be called that. It is a piece of tissue partially closing the external opening of the vagina, and the myth is that it does not break until it is ruptured by the penis when a girl has intercourse for the first time. Thus it is the "maiden's head," and a girl is said to lose her virginity when the hymen is broken. Literature is full of stories about this symbolic piece of tissue, and millions of people in many countries still believe that a man who takes his new wife to bed on their marriage night and finds the hymen broken before they have intercourse can be sure she has already had sexual relations with a man.

In fact, the tissue is often broken in young girls through various kinds of physical exercise, or it may be broken by a girl exploring her own genitals, or by some kind of accident. There are even cases, somewhat rare, in which the tissue is so flexible that sexual intercourse can take place repeatedly without breaking it. Because of the exaggerated importance some people place on the presence of a hymen at the time of marriage, one Japanese gynecologist has recently performed his ten-thousandth surgical operation making an artificial hymen for prospective brides.

There are people who also believe that the hymen closes up the vagina completely, like a cork in a bottle, but obviously that could not be true or menstruation would not take place. The menstrual flow is discharged as easily from virgins as it is from nonvirgins. If a girl today approaches marriage with her hymen still intact, it is common practice for her doctor to cut the tissue after he applies a mild anesthetic to the area. Sometimes the hymen is ring-shaped, called *annular,* and in that case the doctor simply inserts his fingertips to stretch the tissue so that the penis can penetrate without pain or difficulty or shows the girl how to stretch it herself.

Another myth, common among girls, is that the first sexual intercourse "hurts" because the hymen is broken. Actually any pain is far more likely to be the result of fear and of ignorance of the facts about sexual intercourse. If a woman is relaxed and unafraid, as she will be if she has acquired an adequate knowledge of sexual matters, there is no reason why she cannot receive even a large penis quite comfortably, even though she may be sexually inexperienced.

On the other hand, women who are usually, but not necessarily, sexually inexperienced may have at times severe spasm-like contractions of the vaginal muscles, a condition known as *vaginismus,* if they are under emotional stress. Penetration by the penis under these conditions can be extremely painful, or in some cases impossible.

Still another myth about the hymen common among girls is their belief that during menstruation they cannot use tampons, the small menstrual pads inserted in the vagina, without destroying their virginity. This is not true. In most cases, girls who have started menstruation are quite capable of using tampons and may prefer to use them rather than the ordinary sanitary napkins, which are worn outside. There is, in fact, only one way a girl can lose her virginity, and that is by having her vagina penetrated by a penis.

When that happens, the penis goes first through the external parts of the female sexual apparatus which are easily seen in the mirror. This area of the body is called the *vulva,* and it is made up of several parts. One is the *mons veneris,* also called the *mons pubis.* It is a mound of fatty tissue forming a cushion over the pubic bone, and is covered with short, curly hair—the pubic hair. From this mound extend two longitudinal folds or lips, also covered on the outer sides with pubic hair, and these form the outer borders of the vulva. These lips are called the *labia majora,* meaning "major lips," and they are quite fatty too. Their inner sides have certain oil-producing sweat glands, but they are not covered with hair.

Within the boundaries of the major lips are the *labia minora,* or "minor lips," also appearing as two longitudinal folds, running about parallel with the major lips. They come together at the top just below the mons veneris to form the female prepuce, like the male's foreskin, which encloses the *clitoris.* The labia minora are highly sensitive to sexual stimulation. When they are stimulated, they flare outward, but under normal conditions the lips are close together, more or less hiding the inner region of the vulva from view.

The *clitoris* is a small, round, elongated organ located under the upper portion of the labia minora. Like a very tiny penis, the clitoris has a shaft and glans, but it doesn't hang free and only the glans is exposed from under its prepuce. It resembles the penis in another way, too, because its shaft contains erectile tissue, and when it is sexually stimulated, it may enlarge in width to twice or more its nonerect size. The glans of this organ contains a great number of nerve endings, again like the penis, and it is the most sexually excitable part of a woman's body. It responds to both direct and indirect stimulation.

Just as boys can acquire smegma under the foreskin, as I described earlier, so can this smelly, cheeselike collection of genital secretions form under the prepuce of the clitoris. If these secretions are allowed to dry and harden, scratches and irritation can result from the friction between prepuce and clitoris. This condition may cause severe pain when the clitoris enlarges during sexual excitement. Once it was believed that the best way to deal with this condition was to cut back the prepuce by means of surgery, but today the practice is to lift the prepuce from the clitoral glans by using a wooden or metal probe so that the ragged lumps that produce the pain can be removed. Obviously, however, the easiest and best way to avoid smegma is to keep the area washed and clean so that it cannot collect.

Finally, the female sexual apparatus includes the *vestibule.* That is the region enclosed by the labia minora, and in it are the openings for the urethra and the vagina. The urethra, of course, is the tube through which the urine passes from the bladder out of the body. This urethral opening is located about halfway between the clitoris and the vagina.

The vestibule also contains the tiny openings of Bartholin's glands, situated on each side of the vaginal opening. These glands produce a drop or two of fluid at the time of sexual excitement, and it was once thought that the fluid served as a lubricant during sexual intercourse. Recently, however, research has shown that not enough of the fluid is produced to be of any real help, and that the lubrication comes from the vaginal walls, in the way I have described.

So much for the "plumbing," then, of the male and female. It sounds mechanistic to talk about it this way, I know, although the body is often described in the manner I have titled this chapter—as a "marvelous machine." But there is so much more to it than that, so much more to sex than an incredibly complex machine that does our bidding. We are not machines, but human beings. How we come to be so is probably the most astonishing part of the whole sexual story.

Making people: From fertilization to birth

WHEN A MALE EJACULATES during sexual intercourse, from 200 to 300 million sperm are deposited in the vagina. Most of them die in the vaginal tract because the acid condition that is present there doesn't favor their survival. Those that live, however, attempt to move toward more favorable ground, propelling themselves along by lashing their tails. They move toward the opening of the cervix, and from there they progress through the uterus to the Fallopian tubes.

If conception takes place, as I noted in the previous chapter, it will probably occur in the flanged end of one of the Fallopian tubes, and probably it will happen around

29

the fourteenth day of the menstrual cycle. When a sperm meets an egg and penetrates its wall, the process of fertilization is complete. From that moment on, the female is pregnant. The fertilized egg contains in its chromosomes all the characteristics the male and female have contributed to the creation of a new human being. Pregnancy is the word we use to describe what happens in the female's body from the moment of fertilization to the birth of her baby.

"How do I know if I'm pregnant?" Millions of girls have aimed that question at themselves or someone else.

Doctors divide the signs of pregnancy into three classes: first, the individual experience of each pregnant woman; second, the probable signs; and finally, the positive signs. Obviously, the doctor and the laboratory technician deal only with the last two.

But what makes a woman think she might be pregnant? Most of the signs are familiar, part of nearly everyone's common knowledge. A girl misses her menstrual period and her first thought is, "Maybe I'm pregnant." That doesn't always mean it's so. Then she feels nausea in the morning, commonly called "morning sickness," another sign. But again not necessarily; some pregnant women are never sick in the morning, and some nonpregnant ones mistake the nausea of anxiety for the morning sickness of pregnancy. There are other symptoms: changes in the size and fullness of the breasts, a darkening of the area around the nipples, fatigue, frequency of urination. Not all women have these symptoms at the same time, nor in the same degree, and some may never occur at all.

If a girl goes to her doctor, he will be able to detect the probable signs. One is an increase in the size of the uterus. Another is a softening of the cervix, a change that begins during the second month of pregnancy. If she is three months pregnant, the abdomen will show signs of swelling. The expanded uterus can be felt through the abdominal wall, and there are intermittent contractions of the uterus.

There are three positive signs, other than the confirmation from laboratory tests. One is fetal heartbeats, which a doctor can hear and count. Another is active fetal movements, noticeable at the fifth month, although some fluttering movement may be noted even earlier. Finally, an X-ray will show the fetal skeleton.

Most girls, however, don't want to wait several months to make sure they're pregnant, nor should they, in the interest of their own health and the baby's. Consequently, if a girl believes she is pregnant she ought to go at once to a doctor and get hormone tests. They can provide an accurate proof of pregnancy about three weeks after the fertilized ovum is attached to the uterus, or about six weeks after the last menstrual period.

The substance that provides this proof is the hormone secreted by the tissue that connects the mother and the implanted embryo. A sample of urine is used for the test. If traces of this hormone are found in the urine, the girl is pregnant. The question can be decided in a matter of hours, or even minutes, depending on the speed of the laboratory's testing, and the rate of accuracy runs as high as 95 percent, depending on the particular test used and the length of time since the last menstrual period. A word of caution: test results from urine obtained earlier than six weeks after last menstrual period are unreliable if they prove negative, because the hormonal secretion is too slight.

Once she knows she is pregnant, and means to have the baby, the first question a girl usually asks is, "When will it be born?" The prospective birth date can be figured by adding 280 days to the date when the mother began her last menstrual period. It's a fairly accurate method, but to be more exact, she would have to know the actual date of conception, and that is often impossible to determine.

People who rely on the fact that ovulation and conception usually take place halfway through the menstrual cycle, and consequently think they are "safe" in having intercourse before or after, should know that ovulation can take place in an irregular way, on any day of a girl's monthly cycle, even during the menstrual flow itself. Further, some specialists think that even though a girl may ovulate at the regular time of the month, strong sexual excitement may cause her to do so again.

Girls who think they may be pregnant need to have a doctor's confirmation as soon as possible, not only for their own peace of mind, but to be sure they are not having a false pregnancy. It's quite possible to have all the symptoms of pregnancy—missed period or periods, nausea, a significant gain in weight—and to have the condition continue for months when there is no actual pregnancy. A girl might actually go into labor, only to find that she can deliver no more than an accumulation of air and fluids. Emotional factors are the cause of this condition, and it usually results when a girl wants intensely to be pregnant, to have a child—or, paradoxically, when she is just as intensely afraid of becoming pregnant.

There are a good many myths about pregnancy carried over from the past, as there seem to be about every other kind of sexual activity. Until recent years it was widely believed, even by doctors, that travel, exercise and driving a car were all dangerous activities during pregnancy. Now we know they're good for a healthy pregnant girl, if they are done moderately and sensibly, under an obstetrician's direction. Another myth was that a pregnant girl should stop having intercourse for fear she might lose the baby. Now doctors approve and even encourage it, until approximately the final six to four weeks.

While most females have their first babies between the ages of 20 and 24, one little girl who was only 5 is known to have given birth, and, at the other end of the scale, women as old as 58 have had babies. Recent studies show that women past 40, once considered beyond the childbearing age, have as good a chance as younger women of giving birth to a live infant, although it may have to be taken from them surgically by the delivery method known as Caesarian section. When it comes to family size, leaving out birth control by means of contraception, a female can't tell how many children she may have. About one in ten couples is never able to conceive a child at all. The average number of children in an American family at one time is statistically 1.33, but some astonishing records for family size have been set in the world. A Russian couple probably holds the title: 69 children born in 27 pregnancies, including 16 sets of twins, 7 sets of triplets, and 4 sets of quadruplets. The chances of anything approaching these figures happening to an ordinary couple are astronomical.

What happens before a baby is born—the period of prenatal

development from fertilization to the end of the usual nine months of pregnancy—is divided into three periods. As the developing fertilized cell progresses to the second week of pregnancy, it is called a *zygote*. From the second to the eighth week, it is known as an *embryo*. From the eighth week to birth, we call it a *fetus*.

Developing zygotes are especially fascinating, because the fertilized ovum, containing all 46 chromosomes, immediately begins to divide. At the beginning the zygote looks like a sphere, but then it divides into two cells, then four, then eight, and so on until a hollow ball of cells is formed. All this occurs as the multiplying zygote moves on a slow journey through the Fallopian tube, coming to rest finally in the uterus on what is usually the twenty-first day of the menstrual cycle. With all this division, the outer dimensions of the zygote remain the same until the cell mass becomes implanted in the wall of the uterus, where it will be nourished until birth.

Then something quite marvelous happens to the internal cells of the zygote. They develop into three layers of cells, and from these eventually develop all the body's structures and systems. The first layer is the *ectoderm*. Out of these cells grow the nervous system, the sense organs, the mouth cavity and the skin. The second layer is the *endoderm,* and from this comes the digestive and respiratory systems. The third cell layer is the *mesoderm,* out of which come the muscular, skeletal, circulatory, excretory and reproductive systems.

By the twelfth day after fertilization, the zygote has become completely buried within the lining of the uterus. Little finger-like growths, called *chorionic villi,* sprout outward from the zygote and become attached to the maternal tissue, later becoming the *placenta,* the organ that controls the nourishment of the fetus before birth.

Sometimes the zygote implants itself somewhere else than the lining of the uterus. This is known as an *ectopic,* or misplaced, pregnancy. When this happens, it usually occurs in the Fallopian tube, in which case we call it a "tubal pregnancy." It happens about once in every 87 to 250 pregnancies; some investigators use the smaller figure, some say it is higher. It is important for the doctor to diagnose this condition because what usually happens is that the developing embryo becomes too large for the available space, and surgery is necessary to prevent a rupture of the Fallopian tube. At other times, however, a spontaneous abortion occurs and the developing embryo is expelled into the abdominal cavity and is absorbed naturally by the mother's body.

As the embryo enters the third week of pregnancy, structures begin to form around it, designed to house it and protect it, as well as to obtain food and oxygen and eliminate wastes. One of these structures is the *amniotic sac,* more commonly known as the "bag of waters." It is a tough, thin, transparent membrane which grows until it surrounds the embryo completely. This membrane is filled with a clear liquid called the *amniotic fluid.* The developing embryo is suspended in the amniotic fluid by its *body stalk,* a complex connecting structure.

Amniotic fluid has several important functions. For one, it equalizes the pressure around the embryo, protecting it from jolts and injuries. It also prevents the embryo from forming abnormal attachments to the amniotic sac that might result in malformation of the baby. Then, too, it permits the fetus, later on, to change positions, and still later it helps to make childbirth easier by acting as a wedge to expand the cervix.

The placenta becomes the next stage of development. It appears about the fourth month of prenatal life as a red, spongy body, round or oval in shape, and at the time of birth measures from 6 to 8 inches in diameter and ¾ to 1¼ inches in width at the thickest part, and weighs just over a pound. It is composed of both maternal and fetal tissues, and is formed when the maternal uterine tissue and the chorionic villi of the fetus grow together. Now, too, the *umbilical cord,* developing from the body stalk during the fifth week, forms the direct connection between the fetus and the placenta. A fully developed umbilical cord is about 20 inches long. It trails out after the baby when he is born and the doctor cuts it loose from the body. The small part that remains dries up and later drops off from the body, the point of connection being the navel, what we call the "belly button."

Interchange between the mother and the fetus occurs within the placenta. Food and oxygen from the mother's blood vessels diffuse into the blood vessels of the chorionic villi and the umbilical cord, then into the fetus. Carbon dioxide and other waste material from the fetus travel back through the umbilical cord and chorionic villi and are absorbed by the mother's blood, after which they are eliminated through her urine and bowel movements.

The fetus operates as a closed system, as we can see by the circulation of the blood. Both maternal and fetal blood circulate within the placenta, but at no time, during any stage of pregnancy, is there any mixing of the mother's blood with that of the fetus, unless there is an injury to some part of the placenta. In fact, mother and child frequently have entirely different blood types, and later in life neither one would be able to give a blood transfusion to the other.

The walls between the two circulatory systems in the placenta operate like a fine-mesh screen. A red blood cell, for example, which is only about 1/30,000 of an inch in size, is too large to pass through the openings of the walls from one blood system to the other, yet some chemicals and food bodies are small enough to penetrate the walls without difficulty.

This barrier between the two blood systems generally prevents the passage of bacteria and other disease germs from the mother to the fetus, but some substances, like antibiotics and a few disease-causing organisms, like the one that causes syphilis, are capable of it. Consequently, because some drugs taken by the mother *can* be absorbed into the fetal bloodstream, it is unwise to take *any* medication without a doctor's approval, and that includes alcohol, marijuana, heroin, LSD, or the "soft" drugs like amphetamines.

One drug able to cross is thalidomide, with the result, as everyone has read in the papers, that some pregnant women who have taken this tranquilizer have given birth to physically deformed babies. Until recently another danger came from the virus that causes German measles, so that mothers who got this disease during the first three months of pregnancy sometimes produced babies with severe physical deformity or mental deficiency. Now we have a vaccine that eliminates the danger and every woman should have it before she becomes pregnant.

Smoking by the mother is now thought by many experts to be a particular hazard to an unborn child. When a mother smokes, the heartbeat rate of the fetus is affected. Her infant is likely to weigh somewhat less at birth than the baby of a nonsmoker, and the chance for a premature birth is doubled. In at least one scientific study, the rate of death or malformation among infants of mothers who smoked during pregnancy was higher than among nonsmokers.

Babies grow in the womb at an astonishing rate, more rapidly than at any other time in an individual's life. In the twenty years from birth to maturity, a human's body weight will increase approximately twenty times, but in the nine months between fertilization of the ovum and the delivery of a fully developed baby, the increase in weight is about six *billion*fold.

The early part of pregnancy is the period of most rapid growth. From fertilization to the end of the first month, the cell mass increases in weight by about one million percent, and during the second month the weight increase is 7400 percent. Then it drops to an 1100 percent increase during the third month, and to a comparatively insignificant increase of 30 percent during the final month. It drops even more after birth—fortunately, because otherwise the infant would weigh anywhere from 160 to 170 pounds by the time he reached his first birthday.

When they are born, babies vary considerably in size. The two record holders weighed over 27 pounds and were 30 inches long at birth, but of course this is highly exceptional. The smallest surviving infant on record weighed only 1½ pounds. On the average a newborn baby weighs about 7½ pounds and is about 20 inches long.

Nine months, as everyone knows, is the usual length of pregnancy, but it does vary, for several reasons. If a girl exercises strenuously, she will usually have her baby twenty days earlier than a less athletic woman. We don't know why, but brunettes deliver slightly sooner than blondes. Girls are often born from five to nine days earlier than boys. And about 3 percent of pregnancies last 300 days or more. Probably because the placenta is likely to age and wither, the death rate among babies born after an overlong period of pregnancy is about three times that of babies delivered at the normal time; consequently most obstetricians will induce labor if birth has been delayed.

We come, then, to the last act in the drama of creation—birth itself. During the last weeks of pregnancy, the fetus usually turns to a head-down position in the uterus, preparing for birth. Babies emerge from the vagina head first in about 97 percent of cases, but occasionally the buttocks or legs come out first. That is called a *breech presentation*. Once in about two hundred births, the fetus lies crosswise, with a shoulder, arm or hand entering the birth canal first. In that case, the obstetrician must turn the baby during labor, or else deliver it surgically by Caesarian section.

The process of childbirth has a variety of names—parturition, as it is known medically; and also confinement, delivery and labor. It takes place in three stages, as follows:

1. *First stage.* It can be recognized by several different signs. One is the discharge of a mucous plug from the cervix. This plug forms early in pregnancy and acts as a barrier to keep bacteria and other matter which may be in the vagina from entering the uterus, thus reducing the possibility of infection in both fetus and mother. When it is discharged, it is spotted with bright red blood, and is referred to as "the show." Another sign is the rupture of the amniotic sac, or bag of waters, which causes its fluid (a clear, watery substance) to flow from the vagina. Women commonly refer to this sign as "the water breaking." Labor contractions, of course, are the third and most positive sign. They result from powerful contractions of the muscles of the uterus. When the contractions start, they usually occur every fifteen to twenty minutes, each contraction lasting about thirty seconds. The first contractions are relatively mild and rhythmic, but they steadily last longer and increase in strength and frequency.

In this first stage of labor, the cervix opens to enlarge from its normal size (about ⅛ of an inch) to approximately 4 inches, permitting the passage of the baby into and through the 4-inch-long vagina. When the cervix is completely expanded, the first stage of labor has ended. It lasts an average of sixteen hours for first babies and about eight hours in later deliveries, although this varies greatly from woman to woman.

2. *Second stage*. It takes about two hours, in the birth of first babies, from the time the cervix is completely expanded until the baby is born. When the second or third child comes along, the time is about one hour. In some births, the amniotic sac does not rupture in spite of the fact that labor has been in progress for some time, and the obstetrician then has to puncture the membrane.

Every contraction during this second stage pushes the baby downward, eventually with a force equal to 25 or 30 pounds of pressure. The contractions finally occur every three or four minutes, and when they do, the baby is well on its way. To the mother, the contractions may feel as though they began high in the body and then moved around to the abdomen. Between contractions, there is complete relaxation. In this stage, the head of the baby presses on the mother's lower vagina and bowel, causing a tensing of the muscles in that area, which also helps in the birth process.

With each contraction, the infant is pushed along the birth canal until its head appears at the external opening of the vagina. As the head emerges, the tissue between the vagina and the anus stretches to an extreme degree. Sometimes the vaginal opening isn't elastic enough to allow an easy passage of the baby's head, and in that case the obstetrician performs a surgical procedure called an *episiotomy*, which means that he makes a straight cut in the tissue of the vaginal opening back toward the anus. That prevents a jagged tear of the tissue and possible injury to the emerging infant. The incision is easy to sew up again, and it heals rapidly.

Now, in this second stage, the mother may be asked to help to force the baby into the world by contracting her abdominal muscles, commonly called "pressing down," to create additional pressure. The obstetrician may help, too, by applying pressure on her abdomen to help in speeding up the birth process.

As soon as the baby's head emerges, the doctor holds it

with both hands and gently guides it downward, only guiding and never pulling it, while one shoulder emerges and then the other. After the birth of the head and shoulders, the remainder is a simple matter because the trunk and limbs are quite small in comparison with the head and shoulders.

Sometimes the baby is born with too much skin (or so it appears) for his face and head, giving him a wrinkled appearance. That is because the bones of the head, which have not yet fully grown together, overlap and decrease the size of the skull in order to make birth easier. There may be some odd molding of the head, or swelling and bruising of the facial features, but these are temporary conditions. (In breech births, the baby's buttocks and genitals may be bruised.) The head quickly returns to its normal shape, the wrinkles fill out, and the swelling and bruises disappear within a few days. Very rarely is there any permanent damage.

Once the baby's head emerges, the doctor, using an ordinary syringe, removes any blood, amniotic fluid, or watery mucus that may have gathered in the infant's nose and mouth. Some obstetricians still follow tradition and hold the infant upside down, slapping his bottom to help bring about the first breath. But these days most don't consider this old-fashioned procedure necessary, since the change in atmospheric pressure and temperature will usually cause breathing to begin without any help.

When the infant takes its first breath, a drastic change occurs in his circulatory and respiratory processes. (Before birth, as I noted earlier, food and oxygen were supplied by the mother through the placenta and umbilical cord.) Now the same pressure and temperature changes that force the baby to breathe also create a vacuum in the chest cavity, and this vacuum sets in motion the complex circulation of blood, in which oxygen from the lungs is mixed with the blood.

It takes a few minutes for this process to begin and become effective. During that interval, the baby is bluish in color, but as the circulating blood begins to absorb oxygen, he becomes pink. This process seldom fails, but when it does, the result is what we commonly call a "blue baby." Fortunately, modern surgery is able to correct this condition in most cases.

As soon as the infant breathes the oxygen of the outside world, he no longer needs the placenta or umbilical cord. Once the cord stops pulsating, and the baby is breathing regularly, the cord, still attached to the placenta, is clamped and cut about three inches from the baby's abdomen. As I have described a little earlier, the stump withers and falls off in a short while.

3. *Third stage*. This occurs about fifteen minutes after the baby's birth. Additional muscular contractions of the uterus detach the placenta from the uterine wall, expelling it and the remainder of the umbilical cord, sometimes called the "afterbirth," from the body. This stage is very short, usually from three to ten minutes. When it is over, parturition is complete. All that remains to be done is to wheel the mother to the recovery room, if she has given birth in a hospital, and the baby goes to the nursery.

When a girl thinks about having a baby, if she hasn't been told otherwise, the thought uppermost in her mind is the pain of childbirth which lies ahead of her. Generations of girls have been brainwashed into believing that childbirth is an extremely painful experience, which may end in death. Literature is full of childbirth scenes confirming this idea. Motion pictures have added to the impression in extremely vivid ways, and word of mouth has supplied what print and images have failed to provide.

Once all this was simply accepted as a distressing fact of life, and many terrified women suffered in anticipation and in actuality. Now we know that suffering during childbirth is related to the individual mother's past experiences, her prenatal care, how severe she expects labor pains to be, and the culture in which she lives.

Obviously, some discomfort can be expected from the uterine contractions and vaginal stretching involved in the birth of a baby, but extreme suffering is likely to be the result of psychological factors. Understanding of the birth process, confidence in the obstetrician, and security at home, particularly in the relationship with the father of the child, are important factors which determine whether a woman has an easy delivery.

In the last decade or so, the art of relaxation and freedom

from fear has been taught to thousands of women who want to have their babies by "natural childbirth," with the husband present, sometimes at home. When a woman completely accepts and practices this method, childbirth often becomes a relatively easy, even joyous, experience.

Some women, of course, can't accept this method, but for them the art and science of giving anesthesia during delivery has become so refined that there is rarely an excuse for any of the anxiety or pain that many girls associate with childbirth. The obstetrician is able to choose from among many forms of anesthesia, according to the needs of each mother, which will reduce labor pains to a minimum. The argument that is still advanced by some people, including some doctors, that a woman will not love her child unless she experiences pain during delivery is utter nonsense, and should be treated as such. The evidence proves exactly the reverse.

I have described the birth of a single baby, but it's safe to say that when a girl first learns for certain that she's pregnant, the thought crosses her mind at least once, "What if it's twins?"

Well, what *are* the chances? To begin with, births in which more than one baby are born occur about once in 80 to 89 births. Twins occur about once in 80 births, triplets about once in 6400 births, and quadruplets about once in 512,000. Multiple births seem to occur more in some families than others, raising the question of heredity, and other factors appear to involve race and the age of the mother. They occur more frequently in one family than in another, and to more women in their thirties than in their twenties. Studies show that multiple births are most likely to occur in women between the ages of 35 and 39. Black people have more twins than whites do, but whites have more than Oriental women. Triplets are born to whites at a ratio of 1 to 10,200, and to nonwhites at a ratio of 1 to 6200. The difference is the same in both Northern and Southern states, indicating that environmental factors have nothing to do with it.

Identical twins occur when a single fertilized ovum first divides and then, for reasons unknown, separates completely. The two parts continue the process of cell division separately.

Since they develop from the same sperm and ovum, identical twins have identical sets of chromosomes. They are always of the same sex, and share a placenta. In the rare cases where the cell mass doesn't make a complete separation, the result is Siamese twins, joined to each other by a body of tissue.

Twins who are not identical are called fraternal twins. They develop from two separate ova, both of which are fertilized at about the same time by different sperm. A single ovarian follicle may expel two or more mature ova into the Fallopian tube, or else ova in two or more follicles may develop to maturity at the same time. Fraternal twins can be of the same sex, or of different sex. They have separate placentas, and they will look no more alike than separately born brothers or sisters would.

Most twins are born within a few minutes to an hour of each other. For them, pregnancy ends about 22 days earlier than the usual single pregnancy does; the average is about 37 weeks.

Triplets can result from the fertilization of three different ova by three different sperm, in which case they are called fraternal triplets, but more commonly only two ova are involved, one of which separates after fertilization and develops into identical twins. The other fertilized ovum develops normally into the third triplet. In this case, the triplets are a combination of identical twins and a fraternal twin.

Recently, many women who were unable to ovulate have become fertile and had children through the use of fertility drugs. Some of these drugs, however, cause several ova to mature and be discharged during the same ovulation, resulting in a marked rise in multiple births wherever in the world these drugs are used. Some really exceptional multiple births have been reported—as many as seven children on several occasions, eight in one case, and even one of nine. The infant death rate is exceptionally high in all these cases.

In multiple births, the percentage of males decreases as the number of children born at one time increases. A probable explanation is that the female is more likely to survive than the male is, from conception on, in any case, and in multiple births this tendency is simply greater.

Earlier, in describing childbirth, I mentioned Caesarian section as a surgical procedure when the normal process is not possible, and perhaps it needs a little more explanation. Simply, it is surgery in which the baby is delivered by means of an incision in the walls of the abdomen and uterus. The notion that the procedure got its name because Julius Caesar was delivered in this manner is just another myth about sex. Although no one knows for certain, the probability is that the name originated from an ancient Roman law, later made a part of an important legal code called the Lex Caesarea, or "Caesar's law." This law demanded that an operation be performed on a woman who died in the advanced stages of pregnancy, so that the baby's life would be saved.

There was a time when the death rate among women who had a Caesarian section was exceptionally high, not only because of possible excessive bleeding but because of the danger of infection. Today a death following this operation is extremely rare, and a woman may have several babies this way, if she cannot have them in the normal fashion. In fact, it is not all that unusual for a woman to have five or six children by Caesarian section.

So the baby is born at last, and the question of how it is to be fed, breast or bottle, has to be decided.

The process of milk secretion from the mother's breast is known as *lactation*. It begins from two to five days after the infant's birth. In the uterus, the placenta not only provides for the development of the fetus but also produces hormones that prepare the mammary glands in the breasts for this secretion of milk. When the placenta is expelled from the mother's body during the third stage of labor, the pituitary gland, located at the base of the brain, begins to produce the hormone, LTH, that actually triggers production of the milk, which begins to flow soon after birth.

Valuable nourishment comes from the mother's milk. The first secretion the baby gets is colostrum, a high protein substance present in the breast immediately after birth. We don't know exactly what effect it has on the newborn, but scientists believe it provides the infant with some protection against many infectious diseases during the early months of his life.

Sometimes lactation is accompanied by various psychological and physiological symptoms, like fatigue, headache, hot and painful feelings in the breasts, and even low-grade fever. The infant's sucking provides relief for these conditions, and many doctors think this sucking also causes certain muscular contractions of the uterus that help to reduce it to its normal size after childbirth.

Mothers who are breastfeeding their babies can harm the infants by consuming alcohol, strong sedatives, or tobacco. For example, concentration of alcohol is in the same proportion in the milk as it is in the mother's blood.

For a long time breastfeeding became unpopular, after a period in the not so recent past when as many as 90 percent of babies were fed that way. This figure had declined sharply to 23 percent in 1946, and by 1956 it was only 12 percent. In the youth revolution of the Sixties, however, with its emphasis on naturalism in lifestyles, breastfeeding made a spectacular comeback. Without getting into the controversy about it, I can say what is commonly observed, that even though no reliable statistics are yet available, more and more young girls breastfeed their babies today, after a long period in which the bottle was the preferred source. Moreover, as a New York *Times* headline put it in 1973, "Breast Feeding in Public A Growing Trend." Times and customs change.

Some of the reasons for breastfeeding's decline in the past were demolished in the sexual revolution of the Sixties—the idea that it was "animalistic," for instance, and the fear that figures would be damaged. Nevertheless, there are times when breastfeeding is not practical, particularly when a mother has a job or other duties outside the home. Then, too, mother's milk does not agree with some babies, or in other cases mothers become too anxious over whether a baby is getting proper nourishment. In these instances, and others, mothers rely on the many excellent prepared formulas on the market.

Whether or not breastfeeding is advisable is a matter that pregnant girls should discuss with their obstetricians and their pediatricians before the baby is born.

So ends the cycle of creation, then, from fertilization to the feeding of the newborn infant. It has been called a "miracle" so often that the word has become a cliché in describing it. Just the same, it would be hard to find a better word to express the way we feel when we think about this infinitely complicated physiological process. We may be able to grow babies in test tubes some day, and even alter the characteristics of humans before they are born, but we can't begin to equal what the male and female bodies accomplish to reproduce themselves.

4

How children become adults

MOST PEOPLE STILL BELIEVE AS they have for centuries that men and women are vastly different creatures. Beginning with Dr. Kinsey, however, researchers in our time have confirmed the fact that the sexes are very similar. If there is any such thing as a "typical male" or a "typical female," the differences would have to be based more on customs and cultural attitudes than on actual anatomical characteristics.

We have more physiological similarities than we commonly think, including the sexual systems themselves. From the early embryonic stage—that is, from the second to the eighth week after conception—through the mature adult stage of human development, there is a marked similarity both in the structure and function of male and female reproductive systems. Even the genitals of adult males and females have similar structures, although of course they have been modified by growth and development. As Kinsey observed, "In spite of the oft-repeated emphasis on the supposed differences between female and male sexuality, we fail to find any anatomic or physiologic basis for such differences."

How human sexual systems develop is a complicated matter, so you'll have to follow closely. (It will help to refer to Chapter 2 from time to time.) It's worth the effort, however, because I believe you will understand a good deal more about yourself and your relationship to the other sex if you have a fairly detailed knowledge of how you came to be a girl, or a boy.

To begin, the sex organs of both males and females originate from the same physical structure. In the early days of embryonic life, the reproductive system, whether male or female, appears as merely a thickening in the sexual area on the rear outer layer of the embryonic body cavity, and there is no recognizable difference between the two sexes. In time this thickening of the cell mass grows, and the specific organs of the two sexual systems develop and become differentiated, meaning that the organs can now be identified as being either male or female.

Whether a child is going to be a boy or a girl is determined by a combination of chromosomes, those rod-shaped bodies found in every human cell, which contain the genes that determine every human being's hereditary characteristics. When a man ejaculates his average of 200 to 500 million sperm cells at the climax of intercourse, these cells are usually fairly equally divided in their chromosome content between X (female) and Y (male). The ovum or egg that a sperm seeks to penetrate contains only the X chromosome. Since only one sperm can penetrate and unite with the female ovum, an XX or female child will be conceived if that one sperm contains an X chromosome. If it contains a Y chromosome, obviously, the child will be XY, or male.

In their earliest stage after conception, all embryos develop two systems of ducts, or tubes, known as the Wolffian and the

Mullerian. In the male embryo, Wolffian ducts eventually become the male genitals, and in the female embryo, the Mullerian ducts become female genitals. In each embryo, the ducts of the opposite sex never develop and eventually waste away.

From the beginning, the embryo has sex glands, or gonads. When the embryo is about six weeks old, these gonads begin a more noticeable change or differentiation either into male testicles or female ovaries, from which eventually come the sperm or ova that continue the reproductive process.

Some of the other genital glands are also quite similar in male and female. For example, the part that becomes the prostate in males develops into the structure called the Skene's ducts in females. Again, the part that develops into Bartholin's glands in women becomes Cowper's glands in males; both of these contribute fluid to provide lubrication in intercourse.

External genitals in the two sexes grow, develop and differentiate in the same similar ways as the internal structures. In males, the penis and its urethral passage develop in a parallel with the female's clitoris, vestibule and labia minora. In the embryo, these external genitals are first recognizable at about the sixth or seventh week.

In about the fourth week, the front area of the genital region begins to form the vertical urethral groove. Two folds, or swellings, develop along the sides of this groove. In females, these eventually become the labia majora, and in males, the scrotal pouch. At about the tenth week, the male embryo reaches a recognizable stage because the edges of the urethral groove fold and grow together, forming a tube (the urethra) within the penis. Boys can see where these edges have grown together, in what is called the penoscrotal raphe, because it appears in adults as a scar line on the underside of the penis, running from the scrotum to the head of the organ. Once the penis starts growing, it grows rapidly, and by the end of the third month the male urethra is fully formed, with its foreskin over the glans, as I have described earlier.

While a girl's external genitals are less complicated, they are slower to develop. The genital projection that grew into the boy's penis becomes the clitoris in her case. Like the boy's penis, it is her most sexually sensitive organ and it is quite similar to the male organ in structure, although of course not in size. The labia majora and the other structures develop from the labioscrotal swelling, as I have noted before.

In its early stages, the female's urethral groove follows the same pattern of formation as the male's, but in females the groove never closes to form a tube. Instead, part of it deepens to fashion the vestibule, the area surrounding and including the opening of the vagina. The remainder gradually develops into the labia minora.

What controls this whole complicated process by which similar physical structures, in their early stages, become differentiated enough to make humans distinctly male or female? The answer is hormones, produced by the endocrine system from early fetal life. It's important to know what they are and how they work, because they determine how we grow up and become adults.

Let's jump here from birth and infancy, which we've been considering so long, to the age of puberty, when the hormones make us sexually mature. It is the stage of life when sexual reproduction becomes possible and what we call the secondary sex characteristics—meaning voice pitch, the appearance of breasts and pubic hair, etc.—begin to develop. It's at that point that "boys and girls" become teenagers and enter a different world than the one they've known before. It's a time of particularly rapid growth, like that of infancy, and the major changes are physical and sexual.

It isn't simple physical growth alone that brings about these marked changes, although growth is usually evident. We know this because there are many adult men and women who don't have the proper primary or secondary sexual characteristics they need for full sexual ability. At the other end of the scale, there are boys and girls not yet teenagers who are sexually mature enough to father or give birth to babies. The reason for these broad variations, and for normal development as well, is the behavior of sex hormones.

People think of puberty as a "state," but actually it is more of a *change*, more of a "becoming" than being. Differences between the sexes have become more noticeable by this time as the sexual glands mature, and as these differences become greater, girls become women and boys become men, which means they are physically mature.

Since we are a country which likes to classify things neatly, we've always been inclined to believe that puberty begins at 13 and ends at 18, and we call it, again neatly, "adolescence." Actually, it is far from being so cut and dried. The age at which the changes begin and end varies with each individual, so that there is no such thing as "typical" puberty. All we can say, in general, is that girls begin their rapid maturing process at about 10 or 12, or about two years before boys do, and their development is faster. That gives them a temporary superiority over boys, physically and sexually, which means that they may be socially superior too. At 16, for instance, most girls have reached their full height, but boys continue to grow until they are 18 or older.

It isn't height that early adolescents are thinking most about, however. This is a period of sexual awakening, and since the two sexes view this awakening somewhat differently, there is often a conflict of attitudes, which have changed from what they were in the preadolescent period. Emotions and interests change, too, and experimentation and new physical sensations are not uncommon. Boys who have been masturbating from time to time for years now begin to feel an urge to do it much more often. Girls who have never masturbated discover this new sensation and begin to experiment with it.

Girls notice the first evidences of puberty in their breasts. Before, these have been small, cone-shaped buds, but now they begin to increase in size and the nipples start to project forward. The breasts grow in size and sensitivity as the shape of the entire body begins gradually to round out. The bony structure of the pelvis (the hip region) widens and a growth of fatty pads on the hips develops. The lining of the vagina thickens, and soft, downy, rather colorless pubic hair appears around the external genitals. The hair thickens and coarsens in time, becoming curly and dark in color, growing downward toward the area of the vulva and assuming the inverted triangular shape peculiar to women.

About two years after the breasts begin budding, and about a year after the appearance of pubic hair, the monthly uterine "bleeding" begins. This is the first real indication that a girl is becoming a woman. While this usually occurs about the age of 13, there is considerable variation because of individual differences in general health, physical development and hereditary factors.

Many people think a girl is capable of conceiving a baby as soon as she begins to menstruate, but in fact she cannot have a child until she actually starts ovulation, and that process usually doesn't take place until a year or so after menstruation begins. When a girl's ovaries produce their first mature eggs, at about 14, she has reached puberty.

There are exceptions both in the time this physiological maturing begins, and the order in which the changes occur. In 1939, for example, a Peruvian girl gave birth to a normal and healthy son when she was only 5 years of age, although it had to be delivered by Caesarian section. Doctors who examined the little girl described her as sexually mature and confirmed that she had menstruated since she was about a month old.

Even before they experience it, most girls know about menstruation in the familiar phrases, "having your period," and "on the rag." We don't hear another phrase so much these days, but for many years women also referred to it as "the curse." The length of time from one menstrual period to the next is the menstrual cycle. It is measured from the first day of one period until the day before the next one begins. Although the cycle can vary from 21 to 90 days and still be physiologically normal, the average duration is about 28 days (usually longer for young girls), and the menstrual flow itself usually lasts only four or five days during the cycle. In the thirty to thirty-five years a woman is capable of conceiving, she menstruates from 400 to 500 times. She stops during pregnancy, but her periods begin again about four to six weeks after childbirth. If the baby is breastfed, her periods may be delayed longer.

While menstruation can occur even without the discharge of an ovum, the primary purpose of the cycle is to prepare the uterus for the implantation of the fertilized egg. This process takes place in four stages:

1. *Menstruation.* If the ovum is not fertilized, it and its yel-

low body, called the *corpus luteum,* waste away. The lining of the uterus, carefully prepared as a nesting place for the fertilized egg, is no longer needed, so the production of progesterone, the hormone that maintains the uterine lining, stops. This sudden withdrawal causes the lining to break down and slough off, and it is discharged from the body in the form of bleeding, sometimes said to be "the weeping of a disappointed uterus."

2. *After menstruation.* After the menstrual flow stops, the uterine lining is very thin, but stimulated by the hormone estrogen, it begins a process of growth lasting about nine days. There are many follicles containing a developing egg, but usually only one begins ripening to maturity during any one cycle, as I have described in an earlier chapter. This is the Graafian follicle.

3. *Ovulation.* On about the 13th or 14th day of the menstrual cycle, the Graafian follicle ruptures, and a mature ovum is discharged and begins its journey through the Fallopian tube. There is a maximum amount of estrogen in the blood at the time of ovulation.

4. *Premenstruation.* After the release of the ovum, the follicle seals itself off and the yellow body develops in its cavity. This occurs on about the 15th to 18th day of the cycle. The yellow body begins to produce progesterone actively, and the concentration of estrogen begins to decrease. The endometrium of the uterus begins to thicken, and now small lakes of blood begin to form in the uterine wall. If the ovum becomes fertilized and implants itself in the uterine wall, this is the blood that will provide nourishment for it.

Just before menstruation, the breasts usually increase in size and sensitivity, and there is sometimes congestion of mucous membranes in the reproductive system, causing fluid to accumulate and a consequent temporary weight gain that may be as much as five pounds. Then menstruation begins again, and the cycle is completed.

The bloody menstrual discharge lasts from three to seven days; the average is five. It consists not only of blood, but contains other fluids of mucous material and debris from the uterine wall, fragments of the uterine lining, and dried cells from the vaginal walls. Its amount varies from woman to woman, sometimes in the same woman. During the entire flow, however, there is on the average about a cupful of fluid, or six to eight ounces, discharged. But the amount of actual blood loss on even the heaviest day of flow is only about a tablespoonful. There is usually no clotting because the elements necessary for clotting are not present in the menstrual blood.

With the beginning of menstruation, a number of physical and emotional changes may occur, like an increase in the frequency of urination, or in the size and firmness of the breasts, or skin disorders such as pimples. Sometimes there is fatigue, headaches, irritability or nervousness. But these changes are not the inevitable accompaniment of menstruation, as so many people think. They may occur because of psychological factors —negative attitudes toward sex in general and menstruation in particular—or they may have physiological causes. On occasion, both are involved.

How this can happen is easily seen in what occurs as the tissue of the uterus dies and breaks away. The toxic condition of the body increases as the bloodstream picks up some of this material and circulates it. Then, just before menstruation, the decrease in progesterone upsets the balance between estrogen and progesterone. This imbalance can bring about undesirable physical and emotional reactions in some girls.

Girls have all kinds of questions and fears about menstruation, as surveys constantly tell us. Probably the most common is, "What causes cramps?" There is no single answer; several things can cause them. They may result from a uterus slightly out of its normal position, or from one that is malformed or infantile in size. Another cause is a cervical opening that is not large enough or that is blocked. They can also be caused by some inflammation or disease in the reproductive organs. Sometimes good posture and a sensible diet, along with proper rest and recreation, will help correct menstrual cramping that has a physical origin. But only a gynecologist can provide correct diagnosis and treatment if these symptoms persist over a long period of time.

More likely, cramping has a psychological cause. Girls often grow up with unhealthy attitudes about sex, including menstruation, and are weighed down by the emotional feelings of their mothers about these things or by worry or guilt resulting from inaccurate or little sex information. Understanding how and why menstruation occurs should remove the psychological tensions that cause cramping, but if it doesn't, a gynecologist should be consulted to see if the cause is physiological after all.

Like everything else connected with sex, menstruation has acquired its own mythology and superstitions. For example, some girls think bathing, showering or shampooing isn't safe during menstruation. No truth in it. Until fairly recently, it was believed for centuries that exercise was harmful during a girl's period. Now we know that not only is participation in most sports not harmful to the reproductive organs, but that it's much healthier, physically and mentally, for a girl to participate in any recreation that she normally enjoys.

Girls worry about irregularity in their periods, thinking they might be pregnant, if they have any reason to think so, or simply worrying about the irregularity in itself. There are a variety of causes of irregularity. It can be due to hormonal imbalance, or to such emotional stresses as fear, guilt or depression. Again, it may be caused by physical abnormalities—illness, an infantile uterus, malformation of the uterine lining, cysts, or tumors. If irregularity is persistent, a gynecologist should be consulted.

Another old wives' tale is that blackheads, pimples and acne are somehow related to menstruation, or else are the result of sexual activity, especially masturbation. The cause of these troubles is much more complicated. Girls may find that they have a greater number of skin blemishes just before and during menstruation because of the hormonal and uterine changes that occur then, but ordinarily the basic cause of these disorders is either clogged pores or an invasion of bacteria. And certainly masturbation has nothing to do with them!

Girls sometimes want to know if it will harm them to have sexual intercourse during menstruation. Not only is there no harm, but the recent studies of Masters and Johnson show that it may actually provide relief from menstrual discomfort because the contractions of the uterus in orgasm may expel menstrual fluid that may be causing uterine congestion or pressure.

Finally, there are often questions about whether to use sanitary pads or tampons. This choice is purely a matter of individual preference. But the old wives are busy with this one, too, whispering that tampons cause erotic sensations. They don't; the walls of the vagina are insensitive. Another whisper is that tampons are dangerous to the internal genitals. But research shows us that there is no way tampons can harm the cervix, vagina or vulva, not even if they are used when there is an injury or inflammation present. As for the notion that virgins can't use tampons, or that they won't be virgins any longer if they do, I hope I put that one to rest in Chapter 2.

Female sexual changes continue to occur from puberty on into the middle or late teens. The thickened, darkened pubic hair continues to spread. The fatty pads just above the vulva become prominent, and the vulva's outer lips become more fleshy, hiding the rest of that area, which is ordinarily visible during childhood. The inner lips of the vulva also develop and grow. The clitoris develops its complex system of blood vessels rapidly. The vagina turns a deeper red color and its lining thickens and remains so until the *menopause*, or "change of life," when menstruation stops and then it returns to the thinness of childhood. Vaginal secretions now become acid, and the uterus enters a rapid growth period, doubling in size between a girl's tenth or twelfth year and her eighteenth birthday. About 60 percent of 15-year-old girls have wombs of adult size.

When a female infant is born, her uterus is still under the influence of the hormones of her mother, and is larger than it will be until the ovaries start to produce the hormones that eventually cause menstruation to begin. Because of the sudden withdrawal of maternal hormones at the time of birth, the infant's uterus shrinks within a few days after birth, and sometimes the change is great enough to result in vaginal spotting or staining. The uterus of the girl child then remains the same size until her ovaries start their own hormonal production. When she is mature and has been pregnant, the permanent size of the uterus will increase slightly more. When a girl is about 10, her ovaries begin to produce female sex hormones and start to grow rapidly. At the time menstruation begins, the ovaries are approximately one-third their adult size; they reach maximum size and weight at the age of 19 or 20.

In the last few centuries, the age at which girls begin to menstruate has dropped sharply. In Germany, for example, the average age in 1795 was 16.6 years, but by 1920 it was 14.5. In the United States in the late 1930s, the average age at the first menstrual period was 13.5, but figures from the mid-Sixties indicate a drop in this average to 13 years. The age of puberty seems to be leveling off; about half of American girls are believed to begin ovulation between the ages of 12.5 and 14.5. One of the factors which seem to affect both physical growth and date of beginning menstruation is altitude. Girls from Denver, Colorado, for example, have been found to weigh less at birth and to begin menstruating at a later age than do girls from Berkeley, California, at sea level. The oxygen-rare atmosphere of Denver's high altitude apparently causes the lag in development behind the Berkeley girls, although the weight differences disappear when both groups reach the age of menstruation.

Both the prepubertal growth spurt and the beginning of menstruation appear to be determined by body weight, regardless of age or height. The growth spurt tends to begin when a girl's weight reaches an average of 68 pounds, and she begins menstruating when she weighs about 106 pounds. Of course, this is a general finding and there are notable exceptions.

Whenever that major event takes place, the rapidity with which this and other changes, both physical and psychological, occur during puberty may well leave a girl feeling bewildered and insecure. She needs support and guidance from her parents and teachers to help her realize that all the physical changes puberty brings about are normal, healthy processes. It's too bad that teenagers who think everybody over 30 is square and can't be trusted don't realize that there are parents and teachers who can help them through an awkward time. At best, adolescents get through that time somehow, with or without help. At worst, the problems of puberty that are not dealt with sympathetically, and with real knowledge, may lead to emotional difficulties which are bound to have a bad effect on later personal and marital adjustments.

If girls have a difficult time in puberty, it is no easier for boys. Boys' pubertal growth parallels that of girls, but there are differences. In boys, puberty lasts from four to seven years, and the physiological maturing starts later, moves more slowly, and continues longer. A boy's physical superiority does not develop until after puberty; boys of 13 are usually smaller than girls of the same age. But boys today are considerably better developed physically than they were in the past. For example, a 9-year-old boy today is 3.8 inches taller and 18.7 pounds heavier than one living in 1881. If we go back to the beginning of our nation, the average height of men at the time of the Revolution was about five feet, six inches, and George Washington, at six feet, three-and-a-half inches, weighing 265 pounds, must have looked like an early version of a professional football player walking among ordinary mortals.

The most obvious changes in physical size and physiological development are observed first around the age of 12 or 13 and continue beyond the 17th year.

Both boys and girls mature earlier today because of the great improvement in diets and living conditions over those of previous centuries. Some scientists speculate that the hormones frequently given to animals to improve the quality and tenderness of meat being sent to market also have something to do with it, although others dispute this theory. Still another group of theorists think that the "junk" food being consumed in vast quantities by teenagers today is so devoid of real nourishment that the growth and maturity trends of this century will soon be reversed.

Whatever the truth in such matters, it is safe to say that now, as always, boys approach puberty almost cautiously. At 11, a boy shows few outward signs of pubertal change. Boys often have a "fat period" about this time. By the age of 12, the penis and scrotum have begun to show an increase in size, one of the earliest signs of approaching puberty. Erections may occur more often, but while a boy may know about ejaculation, he has yet to experience it.

Pubic hair commonly appears about 13 or 14, and sperm are

being produced at that age, although they may not be mature. Nocturnal emissions, or "wet dreams," occur, even if he masturbates during the day, as most boys do at that age. A boy's voice changes somewhere about his fourteenth or fifteenth year, so that at maturity it is about an octave lower than that of a mature girl. Even so, a boy may not gain his full height and attain mature sexual development until he is of college age.

In both boys and girls, the primary control in sexual maturing is the secretion of sex hormones. They are produced by the endocrine glands, which act like small chemical laboratories, taking materials from the bloodstream, converting them into hormones, and then secreting the hormones directly into the bloodstream, to be distributed through the entire body. The endocrine system is complex, contributing to many of the physiological functions and behavior patterns of humans, but here I intend to talk only about the hormones that more or less directly influence the development, growth and functioning of both sexual systems.

The pituitary gland is of primary importance in the production of certain hormones and in the stimulation of others, although what causes it to secrete these hormones is unknown. It is situated at the base of the brain and is about half the size of a thimble. It consists of three lobes, or parts. Its front lobe, which is known as the "master gland," serves as a coordinator of the functions of the other endocrine glands; consequently it is important to the sexual development, functioning and activity of both men and women. On the other hand, if the pituitary functions abnormally in its role of coordinator, it can have a disturbing effect on any or all of the endocrine glands.

Three pituitary hormones directly control the functioning of the gonads—ovaries in the female, testicles in the male—and so they are called *gonadotropic hormones*. They are:

1. The follicle-stimulating hormone, or FSH. In the female, this hormone stimulates the growth and developmental processes in the ovaries, aids in bringing about the discharge of the ovum from the ovary in the process of ovulation, and influences the production of the hormone estrogen within the ovary. FSH operates primarily in the first half of a woman's

menstrual cycle. It functions in a similar manner in the male to aid in sperm development.

2. The luteinizing hormone, or LH, in the female, and the interstitial-cell-stimulating hormone, or ICSH, in the male. They are identical. LH is the chief stimulator of the hormones estrogen and progesterone, which are produced by the ovaries. It also controls the development of the corpus luteum or yellow body of the ovaries, which is important to early pregnancy. Without ICSH, the process of sperm development, begun under the influence of FSH, would never be completed in the male. It also stimulates the testicles to produce the male hormone testosterone.

3. The luteotropic hormone, or LTH, also called prolactin. This one prompts the secretion of milk by the mammary glands of a woman's breasts after she has delivered a baby.

As I have already mentioned, the male testes and the female ovaries not only produce germ cells (sperm and ova, respectively), but also produce their own hormones, and both these functions are controlled by the pituitary. The testicles produce one hormone, while two come from the ovaries.

Testosterone, the only hormone secreted by the testes, has two functions. It stimulates the development of the prostate, seminal vesicles, penis and associated glands and maintains their proper functioning, and it is also responsible for the development and maintenance of masculine secondary sex characteristics, including facial and body hair, change of voice, muscular and skeletal development, and attraction to the opposite sex.

Estrogen and progesterone are the hormones produced by the ovaries. The Greek word "estrogen" means "to produce mad desire," but in humans this hormone has a more prosaic, though vital, function. It is highly important in controlling body structure, and in the development and functioning of sexual organs. It also influences a woman's menstrual cycle, especially the first half of it.

There is another, and more exotic, effect of estrogen, however. Studies show that women have greater keenness of smell than men, and that the peak of their sensitivity to odors is reached midway between menstrual periods, when estrogen levels are at their highest. In female animals, body odors become much stronger during the estrous cycle, meaning the mating period, and that accounts for the attraction of male animals to them while they are "in heat," as this period is called. Estrogen is responsible for stimulating the sex urge in female animals.

Progesterone, the second of the ovarian hormones, is produced by the corpus luteum, or yellow body, which in turn was stimulated by LH. The corpus luteum is the yellow tissue that fills the small cavity within the ovary (the Graafian follicle) after it has been emptied by the rupture and discharge of the mature ovum when ovulation takes place.

This hormone is of primary importance in preparing the uterus for implantation of the fertilized ovum, and then in the maintenance of pregnancy itself. The bright yellow corpus luteum continues its production of progesterone until about the fourth month of pregnancy, when the placenta takes over the production of both progesterone and estrogen. Progesterone is also necessary to prevent contractions of the uterus that might bring about the premature birth of the baby.

When fertilization doesn't occur, the corpus luteum shrinks away and progesterone production is greatly decreased. In addition, the lining of the uterus is eventually cast off in the monthly flow of blood known as menstruation, as we have seen a little earlier. But then the anterior lobe of the pituitary begins its hormonal production once more, stimulating another crop of ovarian follicles, and the cycle of growth within the ovary begins all over again.

Improper production of progesterone in a woman who is not pregnant may cause difficulties, like painful menstruation and premenstrual tension. If these symptoms are severe enough, a girl needs the help of her doctor.

One of the most fascinating facts about hormone production is that both male and female sex hormones are produced by both sexes, so that there is a small amount of female sex hormones present in the male and a small amount of male sex hormones in the female. The source of the "opposite" hormones is not known definitely, although it is believed that the gonads and adrenal glands are probably responsible. So when you hear it said that each sex has something of the other, it is quite literally true. It can, however, go too far. In adults, an excessive amount of the opposite hormones can produce marked changes in secondary sexual characteristics. Treatment with hormones is often successful in adjusting the imbalance, however, and in turn correcting or preventing related problems.

With the function of hormones, I come to the end of this discussion of the body's physiology, at least in its basic structures. Understanding the reproductive system in both sexes, the process of reproduction from fertilization to birth, and how the sexes develop after birth through adolescence should make it much easier for you to understand the other aspects of human sexuality. I have intended it as a kind of road map. Consequently, now that we know *where* we are, we can begin to talk about the *directions* we may be going.

5

Planning for children

A GREAT OBSTETRICIAN ONCE wrote a book entitled, "Babies By Choice or By Chance," and that is exactly what is involved in the subject of birth control—whether to have children by chance, or whether to plan for them when they are wanted and the parents can take care of them. This is the argument for contraception, the prevention of birth.

People often use the words "contraception" and "birth control" as though they were the same thing, but in reality they are not. To be exact, contraception means any method or device that permits sexual intercourse between fertile partners but at the same time prevents conception. But contraception is only one form of birth control. There are four others, as we will see.

Let's begin with contraception, since it is the most common. There are several different methods, and their effectiveness is measured by their success in preventing pregnancy. Choosing which method to use depends on effectiveness, cost, the degree to which enjoyment of the sex act is affected, and whether the method is morally or ethically acceptable to the individual. If the pregnancy rating of a contraceptive technique is below 10, its effectiveness is considered high. If between 10 and 20, it is considered medium in effectiveness, and if the rating is above 20, we would have to rank it low. The lower the rating, consequently, the higher the effectiveness.

Using one technique consistently is very important to success. Even if it is not considered to be highly effective, when it is used all the time by a couple it is more effective than a "better" technique which is not used consistently. No doubt the worst mistake is the one too many girls make when they don't use a contraceptive the first time they have intercourse, in the mistaken belief that they couldn't be so unlucky as to get themselves pregnant the first time they try it. But the sperm don't know it's the first time, and if the couple are healthy, the chances are as good as though it were the thousandth time and they had been married five years.

Aside from the obvious reason, not getting pregnant, why use contraception? There are five good reasons:

1. *To help a couple reach early sexual adjustment in marriage.* In the early years of marriage, each partner has to learn how to live with the other, which takes a good deal of patience and effort on the part of the young wife and husband. Placing the additional responsibility and demands of a baby on the marriage during this time puts a strain on the marriage that is often too great for the couple to handle. If the fear of pregnancy is removed, however, sexual compatibility can be reached earlier and in a more satisfactory manner. It has also been observed that a wife's ability to respond sexually is directly related to the extent that both she and her husband are satisfied with the method of contraception they use.

2. *To space pregnancies.* Controlling the length of time be-

tween births gives a couple time to consider the mother's health as well as the family's finances. Some doctors believe that when births are only a year apart, the death rate among those babies is about 50 percent higher than it is when they are two years apart.

3. *To limit family size.* For many reasons, most couples prefer to limit the size of their families. One important reason is that having many children may leave the mother in poor physical condition. Equally important is the right of each child that is born to be given proper emotional and physical attention by his parents. There are other factors, too, like the cost of the care and education of children, extremely high these days. Women also don't often want to spend all their young and energetic adult lives being the mother of a baby or small child. By limiting the number of children, and by properly spacing them during the earlier years of marriage, a woman is left with a more leisurely middle age, possibly a more meaningful one. Only 10 percent of women in a recent survey wanted more than four children. And experts in population control warn that our earth is becoming so crowded that every couple should limit the size of their families to two children in order for all human beings to have adequate living conditions.

4. *To avoid making worse an existing illness or disease.* Many physical disorders (like tuberculosis, heart and kidney disease), the advanced stage of diabetes when it may be complicated by damaged blood vessels, emotional disorders, nervous conditions, and recent surgery for cancer make it unwise for a woman to become pregnant.

5. *To prevent the spread of inherited diseases.* Obviously, the spread of inherited diseases can best be controlled by preventing pregnancy if either wife or husband has such a disease.

A large number of medically approved contraceptive devices and products are available today, to be used for any of the reasons above. Let's talk first about those that are available only with a doctor's prescription.

One of the most common is the *diaphragm* with a contraceptive cream or jelly. It has a pregnancy rate of from 4 to 10, which means its effectiveness is high on the scale I outlined previously. The diaphragm is a thin rubber dome-shaped cup stretched over a collapsible metal ring, designed to cover the mouth of the uterus. To be effective, it must be fitted properly by a doctor and used with a contraceptive cream or jelly. The diaphragm itself seals off the cervix and prevents sperm from entering the womb. Because it is poisonous to sperm, the cream or jelly kills them on contact; it is not harmful at all to the girl who is using it. A diaphragm doesn't interfere with the pleasure of intercourse, nor with the act itself.

Diaphragms can be obtained only on prescription by a doctor, and he must fit it the first time, while he instructs the patient in how to use it. This is also done in birth control clinics like those operated through Planned Parenthood. Fitting is of the greatest importance because of individual differences in women. A diaphragm that doesn't fit may be uncomfortable and, worse, will not be effective. Obviously, a girl cannot be fitted with this device until the hymen is broken; consequently there are some doctors who refuse to prescribe a diaphragm until after a girl is married. Others feel differently about it.

The diaphragm can be inserted several hours before sexual intercourse, or immediately before it. It must not be removed until 6 to 8 hours afterward, and can be left in place as long as 24 hours. Douching (washing out the vagina with water) is unnecessary in using it, since the natural secretions of a healthy woman keep her vaginal tract clean. If she still prefers to douche, she must wait at least the 6 to 8 hours following intercourse so that the cream or jelly, or the naturally acid condition of the vagina, will destroy the sperm.

If there is anything to be said against the diaphragm, it is the complaint by some women that it is inconvenient and difficult to use. "Inconvenience" means that these women don't want to invest much time or thought in prevention; "difficult" means that they haven't been taught properly or practiced enough because, in reality, there is no difficulty in inserting a diaphragm. A more legitimate complaint is that it takes some spontaneity out of the sexual act, since the act must either be anticipated and planned for ahead of time, or the natural rhythm of sexual excitement has to be interrupted just before insertion.

There are also some practical disadvantages. Sometimes the

diaphragm fails because of an enlargement of the vagina and movement of the uterus during sexual excitement. It can also fail if, during intercourse, the penis dislodges the diaphragm from its fitted position. Both of these conditions are relatively unusual, however, and the diaphragm has to be given a very high rating for effectiveness.

An entirely different method is the one that has now become a household word, and is known to everyone as The Pill. Physicians call it an oral contraceptive. This method began as early as 1937, when it was shown that the injection of the female hormone progesterone would prevent ovulation in rabbits. After years of further research, a contraceptive pill was finally produced in the laboratory in 1954, and tests were begun to determine its safety and effectiveness. Field tests were made on a large scale two years later in Puerto Rico and Haiti. All these experiments were tremendously successful, and by the late Sixties, drug companies were working overtime to supply the public with a variety of pills under various trade names, while research went on to produce even better ones.

The Pill contains a combination of synthetic hormones. Taken in adequate doses, they prevent ovulation by performing the same function that the natural hormones accomplish during pregnancy. If no ovum is released, obviously pregnancy cannot take place. But the Pill also does several other things to prevent pregnancy. For one thing, the production of gonadotropic hormones is sharply decreased, interfering with the growth and development of the ovarian follicles in which ova ripen to maturity. Then the uterine lining is affected so that implantation becomes more difficult and early spontaneous abortion is more likely to occur if an egg succeeds in being fertilized. The hormones released by the Pill also cause the mucous secretion of the cervix to become thicker. This change aids in contraception by helping to prevent sperm from entering the uterus.

Counting from the first day of her monthly menstrual period, a girl starts taking the pills on the fifth day, taking one a day, preferably at the same hour, for 20 days. Menstruation will start from two to five days after the last pill is taken, although in about 3 percent of the cases, it simply fails to begin. If menstruation does not occur at the proper time, a new round of pills should be started, unless there is a possibility of pregnancy due to skipping a pill. In this case, a physician should be consulted about what to do next.

There are, as always, some disadvantages. One the public doesn't hear much about is the fact that occasionally a woman may lose some of her desire for intercourse after prolonged use of the pills because they interfere with the normal production of certain hormones. But that has to be balanced against the knowledge of being well protected against an unwanted pregnancy with the result that anxiety is removed from both partners; consequently, there is an increase in sexual desire, which is by far the most usual change in sex drive that occurs.

More familiar are the possible side effects of the Pill which have been so often debated in newspaper and magazine stories. So much work has been done to improve the pills since they were first introduced that most of these undesirable side effects have now been removed. When they do occur, usually in the first months of use, the most common symptoms are mild nausea, indigestion, a bloated feeling, an increase in weight, and spotting or irregular bleeding. Other occasional symptoms include abdominal cramping and painful swelling of the breasts. There is no evidence that cancer results from using the pills, even in women who have taken them for as long as six years. The most serious side effect of the Pill is that it increases the risk of blood clotting disorders. Many women have been alarmed by reports that 3 out of every 100,000 women taking the Pill are expected to die from these clotting disorders. What the reports neglect to explain, however, is that women who use other methods of birth control have a 3.5 greater risk of dying from complications of pregnancy, childbirth, and the postpartum period than do women who use the Pill. That's because other birth control methods are so much less reliable than the Pill in preventing pregnancies. If a woman uses no birth control method, the risk of maternal death is 7.5 times greater than it is among women taking the Pill.

If side effects occur, a girl's doctor may well be able to stop them by switching her to another form of pill. A few other precautionary measures can be taken, too. If a woman has taken the pills for 18 to 36 months, there may be some changes in the tissue that lines the uterus; consequently physicians suggest that she take them for a maximum of 18 months at a time, after which she should use another kind of contraceptive for about 3 months so that her natural hormonal balance has a chance to restore itself. Then she can begin taking the pills for another 18 months.

Since the use of a contraceptive pill reduces or stops a mother's milk production, doctors also frequently recommend that she should not take the Pill during the period just after childbirth if she is nursing her baby. There is, too, some evidence that if a mother takes birth control pills while she is nursing a baby boy, the unusual combination of hormones then present in her body can work its way into the baby's bloodstream through her milk and produce some feminizing effects on him.

Not all girls who take the Pill are having sexual intercourse. The Pill can also be used to cure certain disorders, particularly those associated with the menstrual cycle, such as an irregular or excessive flow of blood, and discomfort before or during menstruation.

Girls often want to know, "Why should *I* take the Pill? Why doesn't the man take it?" They will be glad to know that much research is being done in an effort to produce a pill that will cause temporary sterility in men, but so far the side effects have been too severe. The man's sex drive is much reduced, for one thing, and if he drinks anything alcoholic, unusual reactions result. There were obstacles in developing the female Pill as well, and there is good reason to believe those connected with the male Pill will be overcome also and men can then share or take over the responsibility of contraception.

Researchers are also trying to produce a pill to be taken *after* intercourse. It would act for the first few days following intercourse to prevent implantation of the fertilized egg. Another avenue of investigation is being followed to see if it is possible to produce a vaccine that will guard either men or women against fertility for several months. (I might add that animals have benefited from this research—or at least the owners benefit. An effective oral contraceptive for dogs has recently been produced. Administered each day for thirty days before the female comes into heat, it will prevent that period without affecting the animal's ability to produce healthy litters in the future.)

Newer than the Pill are the intrauterine contraceptive devices, known as IUDs, and popularly, if inaccurately, called "the loop." These are small plastic devices of various sizes and shapes, designed to fit into the uterus, where they act to prevent implantation of the fertilized ovum in the uterine wall. Since it is the fertilized ovum that is prevented from implanting, conception has obviously already occurred and the term "contraception" is actually erroneous for this birth control method. A better term would have been "contraimplantation," but let's not quibble.

Like the diaphragm, the IUD must be selected and placed in the uterus by a doctor. It remains there permanently until the user wants to become pregnant, and then the doctor will remove it. After the birth of a child, it can be placed again in the uterus until another pregnancy is desired. The IUD doesn't affect the health of a child that may be borne, nor does it interfere with a woman's ability to conceive at a later time.

As with the other methods of contraception, there are certain disadvantages to using an IUD. It can be expelled without the girl's knowing it, but this is a circumstance that can be avoided by checking it regularly. Two threads hang from the device down through the cervix into the vagina, so that it is possible to make frequent checks to see if it is in place.

Of the several shapes and sizes in which the IUD is available, the best known are the spiral, loop, bow, and ring. Studies of the case histories of 25,000 women who had used the devices for at least a year show that the loop was found generally to be the most effective and comfortable and stayed in place better than the others. But a new T-shaped IUD has recently been developed that is much smaller and easier to insert than the conventional IUD, and has fewer side effects than the loop. The polyethylene T has proved to be almost 100 percent effective. In the past, IUDs could be used only by women who had at least one previous pregnancy but these small IUDs can be used by girls who have never given birth to a baby.

As for effectiveness, IUDs rank among the best contraceptive methods. Work is being done on them constantly, and more doctors are prescribing them for patients than ever before. Their use is increasing rapidly in this country, especially since it has been established that the best of them have a pregnancy rating of about 2 to 3. For a while it was rumored that IUD users were likely to be susceptible to cancer, but clinical tests taken on thousands of users failed to produce any evidence that cancer or any other harmful effect resulted from the devices. Like oral contraceptives, IUDs work for animals too. They are being used by pet owners on their dogs and cats, and even on the sacred cows of India to curb their high birth rate. But actually this is nothing new because for years Arab camel drivers have known to put pebbles into the uteri of their female camels to prevent their becoming pregnant during long desert trips.

There are some contraceptives available without a doctor's prescription, unlike those I've just described. Most familiar, with a history that goes back to antiquity, is the *condom,* commonly called a "rubber," certainly one of the most frequently used contraceptive devices of them all. It is made of strong thin rubber, or of sheep's intestine. At its open end, which is about 1½ inches in diameter, there is a thin rubber ring. The closed end is usually plain, but it may have a pocket to provide space for ejaculated semen, thus decreasing the possibility of its bursting. It usually measures about 7 inches long.

Strict Federal controls have caused manufacturers to improve the condom over the years. Virtually the only drawback to its total effectiveness is the possibility (rare) that it will break during use, or slip off after ejaculation (also rare). In either case, semen may spill into the vagina. Nothing can be done about the former possibility except to inspect a condom carefully before use by blowing air into it. After using, it is advisable to fill it with water to be sure no breakage has occurred. If a condom breaks in use, a contraceptive cream or jelly should be inserted into the vagina immediately, and if that is not available, the girl should douche with water, which is capable of killing sperm. (As you will see, however, douching is a notoriously poor method of contraception.) As for the possibility of the condom's slipping off after ejaculation, the male partner would be well advised to withdraw and take off the condom as soon as possible after orgasm, holding onto the condom while withdrawing.

Perhaps the best reason for using a condom is to prevent the spread of venereal disease, and that may be the major reason, aside from its relative inexpensiveness and availability, that it is the most frequently used birth control method. About 750 million condoms are produced in the United States annually.

Some men object to the condom, no matter what it is made of—sheep gut or rubber—because they say it decreases pleasurable sensations. Another disadvantage is the necessity to stop in the middle of increasing sexual excitement in order to put it on. Its pregnancy rate is a little higher at best than that of the IUD, ranging from 6 to 19, depending on the quality of the rubber.

Another form of nonprescription contraceptive is the whole range of creams, jellies and vaginal foams which constitute chemical contraception. These methods have two basic functions: they block the entrance to the uterus and they contain a chemical capable of killing sperm. Again, there is the interruption problem. They must be put into the vagina about 5 to 15 minutes before ejaculation occurs.

Other chemical methods include the vaginal suppository, a tablet that melts when it is placed in the vagina. Chemicals contained in these tablets can also kill sperm on contact, and their pregnancy rate runs from 5 to 27.

Finally, among the nonprescription methods, there is the douche. In douching, a syringe bag which has a hose and a nozzle that fits into the vagina is filled with water. The nozzle is inserted into the vagina and the water flows out, washing the vaginal walls. The theory behind douching, as a contraceptive, is that semen can be washed out of the vagina before it has a chance to enter the mouth of the womb. In reality, however, sperm move so quickly that the douche usually fails to reach them, and so douching is not considered to be an effective method, which is reflected in its high pregnancy rate of

36. It cleanses the vagina but it does little to prevent pregnancy. Girls should be warned that douching with a bulb type syringe that sprays the vagina with water when the bulb is compressed may cause unexpected difficulties. Many physicians believe that the pressure may force water and vaginal secretions into the uterus, causing irritation of the uterine lining and Fallopian tubes.

I have described the most popular and effective contraceptives on the market, although there are others available. There is one thing to remember. No method is absolutely safe, and recent studies of contraceptive effectiveness prove it. The women in these experiments used contraceptive products (not including pills) according to the manufacturer's instructions. Samples of content were taken from various parts of the vagina several times and examined for live sperm, from 15 seconds to 5 hours after semen was introduced. None of eight products tested was given a perfect score, because every time samples of vaginal content were taken, some live sperm were found. Further evidence disclosed that even a chemical highly effective in killing sperm was not effective if the substance containing it did not dissolve or spread properly within the vagina. Thus a chemical might be very effective in a suitable foam, but ineffective in a jelly, cream, or tablet.

No doubt you've heard the old joke about the absolutely perfect contraceptive—a glass of orange juice, not before or after intercourse, but instead of. That is an accurate description of abstinence, which is the most effective method of preventing pregnancies, but certainly the least popular among married couples for obvious reasons. Since we have been given a complex system to experience and enjoy sexual intercourse, one of the most satisfying experiences in human life, it seems contrary to human nature to avoid it entirely within marriage. In the rare situation where a married couple feel that the only birth control method open to them is abstinence, they are left with only two choices. One is to have intercourse but to live with the ever-present possibility of a pregnancy that for one reason or another is unwanted or dangerous. Or they can avoid intercourse, accepting the fact that not only will they miss all its pleasures but that they are closing off

unequaled opportunities for developing a close, warm, physical and emotional relationship.

Some people have argued that abstinence is valuable because if sexual outlet is limited, performance and productivity
in other areas are the beneficiaries of all this energy and both
will improve and increase. There is no scientific evidence to
support this notion.

Sometimes, of course, abstinence is simply a matter of consideration for the other person, or even oneself—for example,
during an illness, late in pregnancy, immediately after childbirth, or to prevent spreading venereal disease when one
knows it is present. Such voluntary abstinence is less damaging to normal functioning, and the sexual drive can be satisfied
with masturbation, or involuntarily in "wet dreams" (or nocturnal orgasms).

Not many married people want to practice abstinence as a
method of birth control, but for those who object to the
methods I have been describing, for religious or other reasons,
there are two other means designed to prevent conception—
withdrawal, and what the Catholic Church calls the "rhythm
method."

Withdrawal, or *coitus interruptus,* to give it its proper Latin
name, means simply that the male withdraws his penis from
the female's vagina just before he ejaculates. It is probably the
oldest form of birth control known to man, and is even mentioned in the first book of the Bible (Genesis 38:9). It is popular with young people who are too careless, too uninformed or
too frightened to use anything else, and many married couples
use it too. The common belief that it will cause premature
ejaculation if long continued is not true, but there is less
agreement on whether it is reliable as a birth control method.
The chief objection is that the first few drops of the ejaculation contain the great portion of the male sperm. If the man is
slow in withdrawing, and if any of this first ejaculation enters
the vagina, conception may well occur. Further, the few drops
of precoital secretion from the Cowper's glands may collect
sperm cells from the urethral tract, and these can ooze into
the vagina even though the male withdraws his penis before
he actually ejaculates.

But that is not the only objection to withdrawal. At the time of ejaculation, a man's sexual movements are very much different from the movements of withdrawal. That means the man must control the timing of his sexual activity so that his withdrawal is just before his ejaculation—an act that requires strict self-control at the moment of greatest passion and abandon. He is also taking a long chance if he reenters the vagina before a considerable period of time has elapsed after ejaculation, because of the presence of sperm in the urethra from the previous orgasm. With all these factors considered, the pregnancy rate in withdrawal is from 8 to 40, depending on the care and timing of the man.

The rhythm method has a pregnancy rate of 14. The theory behind this method of birth control is based on the generally accepted belief (although authorities differ) that an ovum lives approximately only 24 hours after ovulation unless it is fertilized. Sperm which enter the uterine tubes remain alive and are capable of fertilizing the egg for about 48 hours. Consequently, there are usually only three days in a month when a woman can become pregnant, and the rhythm method seeks to pinpoint the exact three days. If that could be accurately determined, it would be a very good method and couples would feel free to have intercourse without danger of pregnancy on the other days.

Unfortunately, accuracy is what is lacking. In general, the average woman releases an ovum 14 to 16 days before her next menstrual period is due. If she menstruates every 28 days, she should ovulate midway between the two periods, or about the 13th to 15th day after the first day of menstruation. The trouble is that different women menstruate on different schedules, so to determine which are the fertile "unsafe" days and which the infertile "safe" days, a careful written record of menstruation would have to be kept for twelve consecutive months, after which a gynecologist would have to be consulted to make the correct calculations.

Even if that were done, about 15 percent of all women have such irregular menstrual periods that they can't safely use the rhythm method at all. After childbirth, in any case, the first few menstrual cycles may be very irregular and of course the rhythm method will be very unreliable if it is used then. Besides all that, some women may ovulate more than one time during the month. It is also possible for sexual excitement itself to bring on ovulation.

Another way of trying to find the "safe" period is the temperature method. It is based on the fact that there is a relationship between changes in body temperature and the time of ovulation. A woman's temperature is ordinarily relatively low during menstruation itself and for 8 days afterward, 13 days in all. At the time of ovulation, midway in the cycle, there is a dip in temperature and then a sharp rise of ½ degree to $\frac{7}{10}$ degree. This elevation continues for the remainder of the cycle, then drops one or two days before the onset of the next period.

To achieve any kind of accuracy in determining her "safe" period by using this method, a woman would have to take her temperature by mouth, preferably when she first awakens, every morning for six to twelve months. The main difficulty in determining a "safe" period for intercourse by the temperature method is that in some women the changes in temperature may be too slight, or they may vary from day to day. Another problem is that more than one ovum can mature during any one cycle, and research also indicates that the period of time between ovulation and the temperature rise can vary up to four days.

It is not impossible to produce a temperature chart that offers some measure of reliability, but obviously it is not easy to do and few women would take the time or trouble to do it. Rhythm by the calendar is easier but even less certain, so high marks can't be given to the rhythm method and only those whose religious beliefs demand it are likely to practice it faithfully.

We come now to the really drastic methods of controlling conception, sterilization and abortion. Both of these methods have long been involved in emotional controversy but the controversy has been given new life by cultural and political events.

Sterilization is a surgical procedure by which a person is made sterile, that is, unable to produce a child. In the United

States, it is estimated that sterilization is performed in one out of every ten marriages. Today, in contrast to the past, the procedure is performed many more times on men than women. Contrary to popular belief, sex desire is not decreased by sterilization. On the contrary, sex desire often increases because of the freedom from anxiety resulting from the removal of pregnancy fears.

Most sterilization operations are sought by married couples, for economic or social reasons—they feel they are not able to support another child financially, or they don't want to be burdened by children in the later years of their lives. Physicians are sometimes reluctant to carry out the procedure because of the uncertain legal ground on which they stand; they know that some people who plead for sterilization and have it done change their minds later and sue the physician.

There are four ways to sterilize women. One is the surgical removal of both ovaries, or *oophorectomy.* Since this operation removes the source of certain hormones as well as stopping ovulation permanently, the side effects can be quite undesirable, including physical changes toward masculinity and other disturbing physical symptoms. Hormone therapy usually corrects these conditions, however. The second method is to "tie the tubes." It is major surgery, but not especially dangerous or complicated. The Fallopian tubes are simply cut and tied so that the two ends are prevented from rejoining, keeping sperm and ova apart. This is the method of sterilization used on American women when they want the operation simply to prevent a pregnancy and when no problems with ovaries or uterus exist. About 1 in 200 of these operations is a failure and pregnancy occurs.

A third method is widely used in Japan but not well known here. It is called *intrauterine coagulation of the uterine tube outlet,* and consists of applying a special instrument to the point where the Fallopian tubes and the uterus join, cauterizing the tissue and causing scar tissue to form which seals off the tubular openings, thus preventing sperm and ova from coming together. The effect is permanent.

The fourth method is the most common, *hysterectomy,* in which the uterus is removed. Also one or both ovaries and one or both tubes may be removed, depending on the surgeon's view of the pressing needs of the woman. Although its effect is to sterilize, it is seldom performed for that reason alone, but usually to correct certain abnormalities, like fibroid tumors. For a time it was an operation performed so often that it even became fashionable in some quarters, but more recently doctors have been less ready to perform panhysterectomies, in which uterus, tubes and ovaries are taken. They are more likely to remove only those parts which either are already diseased or otherwise threaten the patient's health.

Sterilization in the male is accomplished in only two ways, vasectomy or castration, and only the first is common. *Vasectomy* is the surgical procedure of cutting and tying the tubes that carry the sperm from the testicles. A small incision is made on each side of the scrotum and each of the two tubes is lifted out so that about an inch can be cut out of each. Then each end of the tube is tied, thus preventing the sperm's passage from the testicles to the ejaculatory ducts. The incision is made well above the testicles, and in no way harms them or their functioning. After a vasectomy, a man continues to ejaculate as he always has. This ejaculate is exactly the same, but now it contains no sperm. The sperm continue to be produced, and are simply absorbed by the body.

This is a simple operation, performed in a hospital or even a doctor's office under local or general anesthetic—so simple that it is now being widely advocated as a means of birth control for couples who don't plan to have any more children.

While there is no danger to the male if he follows the doctor's orders of relative inactivity immediately after the surgery, there are other minor hazards. He remains fertile for several days following surgery and his first 6 to 10 ejaculations will contain sperm previously stored in the ejaculatory passages. In some cases, too, the cut ends of the tubes somehow manage to rejoin in spite of all the surgeon's skill, although this is rare. In other cases, an "extra" tube may exist and the doctor not discover it during the operation and the sperm may still have an outlet.

If a man decides after a vasectomy that he wants to father a child, a second operation can be performed to rejoin the ends of the tubes so the sperm can pass through them again. Until recently, this operation was only about 30 to 50 percent successful, but newer techniques are now giving hope for much better results.

Many women argue, with some justification, that selfishness is the chief reason why so many men have refused to undergo this operation, even though it is simpler, quicker, cheaper and less dangerous than the similar operation performed on women. There may be a more subtle reason for male reluctance, however, and that is the fear of losing sexual drive or desire. Even among men who understand intellectually that a vasectomy puts them in no such danger, the fear persists, possibly because the idea of a surgeon's knife being anywhere near the testicles causes the ancient fear of castration to rise up to haunt them. This fear is, of course, unfounded. A man may find, in fact, that his sexual vigor is increased because he doesn't have to fear that his semen will cause a pregnancy.

Castration, an ancient method of sterilization in which both testicles are surgically removed, also has some ancient myths clinging to it. People still believe that the eunuchs of the harem, famous in song and story, were castrated so that they could not have intercourse with the wives when the sultan was not there. In fact, castration doesn't necessarily mean that a man is unable to have and enjoy sexual intercourse, even though there is a gradual loss of sexual desire over a period of time as the result of a loss of male hormones from the testicles. The sultans were worried about the fathering of children, not intercourse. But there are physiological changes following castration, including a change in voice pitch to the higher ranges, a decrease in beard growth, and the formation of excess fat. Today, however, these results can be corrected with proper hormone therapy. But nothing will make the man fertile again.

Castration is never employed as a means of birth control, but is permitted by law in 28 states (and in a qualified way in others) for eugenic reasons. Thus, in some states mentally defective people, those with severe emotional disturbances, or even those convicted of some types of criminal behavior can be sterilized on the theory that their children might inherit their undesirable characteristics, a possibility disputed by most scientists.

Now we come at last to the method of birth control which has been the subject of so much emotional debate in the United States over the past few years—abortion. The debate appears to have been ended in a legal sense by the Supreme Court's ruling that the states may not pass laws forbidding abortion in the first three months, and they have only a qualified right to do so thereafter.

In spite of all the words written during the controversy, millions of girls seem to be uninformed about the basic facts of abortion.

To begin by defining it, abortion is the spontaneous or induced expulsion from the uterus of an embryo or fetus before it has reached a point of development at which it can survive. That point is generally considered to be attained at the twenty-fifth week of fetal life. If the embryo is expelled as the result of an intentional act to end a pregnancy, we say it is an *induced abortion,* and since it is a purposeful act, it is a form of birth control. If there is an accidental or unintentional miscarriage, doctors call it a *spontaneous abortion,* and this is *not* a form of birth control.

A wide range of nonmedical techniques has been used to induce abortion, most of them quite useless and many very dangerous. In their desperation, girls have had other people jump on their abdomens, they have used sticks or some other kind of uterine probe, and they have taken varieties of fraudulent "medicines" made from various chemicals, animal secretions, dung, herbs, and seawater, not to mention the use of magic and mystical chants. Various kinds of medication have been used, including castor oil and ergot, and violent physical exercise, like jumping off a height. Before the recent liberalization of abortion law, those who could afford it and knew where to go, went to illegal abortionists, not many of whom were competent; the resulting death rate and physical damage were high in this $350-million-a-year business.

Pills advertised to correct menstrual irregularities are frequently taken in the hope of inducing abortion. These pills are usually extremely strong laxatives, containing drugs which also act on the uterus. Such strong medication can, and sometimes does, produce severe poisoning, leading to blindness and other permanent disabilities. Any medication strong enough to produce an abortion would also be a severe danger to the life of the woman taking it. Strenuous physical exercise, like jumping or lifting unusually heavy objects, is just as ineffective and may be extremely harmful.

Most people think that unmarried girls are mainly the ones who seek an abortion and get it, but the fact is that about one-half of all abortions are performed on married women. It is estimated that at least 22 percent of all married women have undergone at least one induced abortion. In the past, when these abortions have been performed legally, they were called *therapeutic,* and were undertaken when the patient had a serious cardiac condition, tuberculosis, certain kinds of malignancy, diabetes, some kinds of kidney disease and certain types of mental illness. Such therapeutic abortions are also sometimes done if the woman comes down with German measles during the first three months of pregnancy, or when, in certain cases, the Rh blood factor is present, and also in some hereditary disorders.

Whatever the reason, abortion is usually performed by one of three common techniques.

1. *Dilation and curettage,* popularly known as a "D and C." This is the procedure often used when pregnancy has not gone beyond the twelfth week. The opening into the uterus is stretched with a dilator, and then a spoonlike instrument, a curette, is used to scrape the embryo or fetus from the uterus. It is the same procedure used by gynecologists for a variety of other reasons besides abortion, and is perfectly safe if it is done by a competent physician.

2. *Vacuum method.* In this recently developed procedure, a tube is inserted into the uterus and a vacuum pump is used to suck out the embryo and other uterine content. The technique is safe and is easier and faster to perform than the D and C, thereby causing the patient less trauma.

3. *Menstrual regulation.* This is not, technically speaking, a method of abortion. Instead, it is a method of bringing on a delayed menstrual period. Without pain or bothersome side

effects, the procedure can be performed in a doctor's office in about two minutes. A thin plastic tube is inserted into the uterus and the month's menstrual lining is sucked out with a specially designed suction syringe. Obviously, if a fertilized egg happens to be present, it will also be sucked out, but since this procedure can only be performed within the first 2 weeks of a missed period, there is no way of determining if pregnancy exists. A woman who does not want to have a child should therefore have this procedure performed as soon as possible after missing her period.

4. A new method has been developed in Sweden for abortion after the third month of pregnancy. A hollow needle is used to withdraw about 6½ ounces of amniotic fluid through the wall of the abdomen. The fluid is then replaced with an equal amount of a salt solution, and abortion will occur of itself, usually within 24 hours.

The legal aspects of abortion have now been settled by the highest court in the nation, but the moral argument goes on. Without getting into that argument, which is not within the province of this book, I can only say that a girl who wants an abortion is now able to get one legally and relatively cheaply. If that is her decision, she needs only to be sure that she puts herself in the hands of a competent physician, as she would if she were having any other kind of surgical procedure. She should avoid like the plague having anything to do with illegal operations, which still persist in states where laws governing abortion after three months make legal ones hard or impossible to get. In these cases, agencies such as Problem Pregnancy provide information about where a girl can travel to get a legal abortion. I hope it goes without saying that, in any case, she must avoid every kind of self-induced abortion, no matter what her friends tell her, or whatever the circumstances may be. There is no reason now for girls to kill or injure themselves out of desperation at the thought of having an unwanted child. They are now able to have a legal, and safe, abortion.

6

VD: It's worse than a bad cold

BEFORE THE ANTIBIOTICS WERE developed and markedly reduced the incidence of VD, the wise saying among the young about venereal disease was that "it's no worse than a bad cold." While that was never true, it did seem more plausible when penicillin and other antibiotic treatment produced quick cures of these diseases. For centuries venereal diseases have plagued the world's population, leaving a trail of damaged lives and bodies and earning for one of them, syphilis, the title of "the great killer."

Now we live in a time when VD has, in the opinion of some medical authorities, reached epidemic proportions in the United States, and while the antibiotics are still doing their job, strains of the VD viruses have developed which are highly resistant to them. And suddenly VD is a problem again.

Syphilis and gonorrhea, the two chief venereal diseases, are almost always acquired by direct sexual contact and not from toilet seats, as many people believe. The organisms that cause them are ordinarily found only in human beings, and cannot live long outside the body. These infections attack men, women and children alike, and although we know it is possible to control them, the effort is hampered by the failure of the government to provide enough funds for public health agencies, and by the failure of many doctors to report new cases of VD among their private patients, particularly if they involve adolescents, among whom the incidence is highest. Another obstacle is the natural reluctance on the part of both adults and teenagers to reveal their sexual contacts or, in many cases, even to seek treatment.

Why do an increasing number of teenagers have VD? Beyond the reasons I've cited above, studies by public health agencies tell us something more about the problem. First, it is universal—that is, VD affects all personality types and all levels of society. Clinics report a high incidence among those who come from low-income, minority-group families, but those reports would be expected since people in these groups are the ones who must go to clinics for treatment; others are treated by private physicians, and there the statistics are less reliable. Those statistics we have, overall, show that most of the infected teenagers had begun high school but only 15 percent had graduated; a few were attending college. About 25 percent attended religious services, and 50 percent of their parents did so.

Most parents think VD is the result of promiscuity, but the surveys show that the infected group was no more promiscuous than other teenagers. The higher rate among nonwhites seems to be another by-product of ghetto living conditions. VD is more common among boys than girls, but no doubt that is because the boys have more opportunities. (Promiscuity and homosexuality are also more common in boys.) The studies show an extremely high rate of VD among male homosexuals, but not among lesbians, and in fact the greatest increase in recent years has been in homosexual and adolescent groups.

But the most significant fact uncovered in the public health studies was that teenagers with VD came from families whose members lacked healthy relationships with each other, and who were not united by bonds of mutual understanding and confidence. Only 21 percent of the teenagers studied had been given any sex education by their parents; 64 percent had gotten it from boys and girls their own age. The adolescents who had been given sex education by adults who were meaningful to them showed less tendency to promiscuity.

All the teenagers in the studies lacked adequate information about sex, including VD, and all were extremely ignorant of the basic facts of biology and hygiene. All of them lacked a genuine concern for school or work, but they had feelings of religious conflict and guilt over their sexual activity.

Venereal disease patients almost always see themselves as worthless, unlovable victims of some force over which they have no control. When they are seriously depressed by these feelings, they seek relief in irresponsible sex relations. The American attitude that links security with love, and love with sex, accounts for their attempts to correct their emotional problems by acting them out in their sexual behavior. When they are helped to have a better opinion of themselves, their general adjustment to life also shows a great improvement.

Because of these and other attitudes it is hard for individuals, as well as society itself, to face up the reality of VD when it appears, and that is too bad because the old saw is right in a sense about one thing: most cases *are* easier to cure than the common cold, if a doctor's help is sought early enough. If you have even the slightest question about whether you or your partner has VD, intercourse ought to be avoided, or at least condoms should be used, and a doctor should be consulted at once. You don't have to worry about the doctor calling your parents. He will respect your confidences. If you can't afford a private doctor, go to the public health clinic in your city. However, if your parents will read and discuss this book with you, they are very likely the type of parent who will be understanding and will help you when or if you get into *any* trouble, including sexual.

There are many kinds of venereal disease, but since syphilis and gonorrhea are the most common, let's talk about them first. Syphilis designates a disease that was well known long before it was called by that name. People knew it as "the great pox" until a doctor named Fracastoro published a poem about a shepherd named Syphilis who had the disease. The poem became so popular that somehow the unfortunate shepherd's name became attached to the "great pox" and it became known as syphilis.

It was believed for a long time that Columbus and his sailors brought syphilis to the New World, but studies of the bones of American Indians have shown that syphilis existed in America at least 500 years before Columbus arrived, so it is quite possible that the sailors contracted the disease from West Indian women and took it back to Europe, where it was already a very old story. Columbus himself died in 1506 probably from general paresis, a neurological disorder resulting from syphilis. It was four hundred years later, in 1905, before the organism which causes the disease was isolated, and some time after that when the relationship between syphilis and general paresis was recognized.

When it was discovered at last, the organism turned out to be a corkscrew-shaped spirochete, or bacteria, known as *Treponema pallidum*. It is a cylindrical body with 8 to 14 rigid spirals. Once it was identified, detailed studies were made and effective methods of diagnosis developed, notably the Wassermann test, but it was not until 1943, when penicillin was discovered to be a quick and easy cure, that medical science had a real weapon to deal with the disease. Until then, the best treatment took two years or longer.

Penicillin remains today the most common drug for treating syphilis. It can cure practically any case, if caught in time, and in many instances, only a single powerful injection is necessary. If the patient is allergic to penicillin, Aureomycin or Terramycin can be used with equal success.

Syphilis is considered to be in its early phase for a two-year period after infection, and early syphilis is subdivided into primary and secondary stages of infection. It is highly important to recognize the disease in this early phase, because it is then that it can be most easily cured. It is also the period when the patient is most infectious, and is the greatest menace to public health.

The primary stage is easily identified by a chancre, or sore, that usually appears in the anal-genital area following sexual contact with a diseased person. In about 10 percent of the cases, the sore may appear in the mouth, or on the tonsils or lips, and in those cases may come from a source other than sexual contact, such as kissing a person that has a chancre on his lips or in his mouth.

This primary sore begins as a small red papule, meaning a circular elevation of the skin, that becomes eroded and moist. At this stage the only other sign of infection is a swollen but painless gland in the area where the sore appears. For example, if the sore is on the penis or labia minora, the glandular swelling will be in the groin.

During this early stage, the syphilis bacteria leave the bloodstream and invade various tissues of the body, an invasion which usually causes the breaks in the skin that are characteristic of the secondary stage of syphilis. If the disease is properly treated in its primary stage, it is easy to cure and the danger of passing on the infection is removed. Without treatment, the primary sore heals in 4 to 10 weeks; consequently the external warning signal is removed—a dangerous circumstance, because the danger of internal damage remains.

In the secondary stage of the disease, there is a rash on the skin, usually on the trunk of the body. It is sometimes so slight that it goes unnoticed. But other symptoms also appear about this time—glandular enlargement, throat infection, headaches, vague feelings of illness, and a low-grade fever. The rash and secondary-stage lesions heal without treatment in a few weeks or months, possibly a year, and leave no scars. Since all the symptoms listed above are also symptoms of other, more common ailments, it is possible for syphilis to escape detection even in this second stage. In fact, its resemblance to other diseases at this stage once led it to be called "The Great Imitator."

The third stage of untreated syphilis is called the latent period. It begins at least two years after the victim first becomes infected, and it is dangerously deceptive. All symptoms associated with the disease disappear, and the latency lasts for months or years. Because of this, people who suffered from it in the great syphilis epidemic which swept Europe in the fifteenth century thought they were cured. During the latency period, syphilitics (as they are called at this point) do not infect others, but the results of a blood test are always positive, and such a test is the only reliable diagnosis. If there is still no treatment, the disease advances to the really destructive stage of late syphilis.

Evidence of this stage may appear as late as 30 years after the original infection. It can appear in any organ—in the central nervous system, in the blood vessels, particularly on the skin, and also in the mouth, throat and on the tongue. These late lesions are responsible for the crippling, disabling and disfiguring effects associated with syphilis. Constant inflammation may develop in this stage, affecting bones, joints, eyes and other organs, and especially the heart, brain, and circulatory system.

While modern methods of diagnosis and treatment have made syphilis much less of a major threat than it once was, untreated cases can still produce highly distressing or even fatal results. These are not inevitable, however. Even among persons who have contracted syphilis and have been given no treatment, about half will experience no disability or inconvenience.

The number of cases of congenital syphilis—that is, syphilis that a baby has when it is born—has been greatly reduced by improved prenatal care and treatment of mothers. A syphilitic mother usually passes the disease on to her unborn child if her pregnancy occurs during the first two years of her infection, but if the mother is treated before the fourth month of pregnancy, the child will probably be born free of syphilis.

Symptoms of congenital syphilis can usually be recognized early in the child's life. They are similar to those of the second and third stages I have just described. There may also be various degrees of mental deficiency, ranging from a mild retardation to imbecility and idiocy, as well as other developmental defects, especially in the central nervous system, eyes, heart and other vital organs.

Untreated syphilis may cause major disabling disorders. The

two most common are neurosyphilis and general paresis. In the past, about 5 percent of all untreated cases ended in general paresis, but recently the figure has dropped to about 3 percent, although the exact cause of the decrease is not known. It is a progressive disease with some physical symptoms and many of the psychological symptoms of severe mental illness. Its signs do not usually appear until 10 to 20 years or even longer after the primary lesion of the disease first appears.

General paresis may affect any or all areas of the nervous system, and it is often fatal. Changes in the pupils of the eyes and a positive blood test are often the only indication that a person has it, but if the severe psychological symptoms are present they are dramatic enough, including alternate manic and depressive behavior, anxiety, insomnia, hypochondria, fatigue, irritability, loss of interest, and a loss of concentration.

Neurosyphilis presents most of the same symptoms, although it may develop without any symptoms that can be observed, but it appears to result mostly in a long list of personality disorders.

Gonorrhea is better known by the word "clap." It is the oldest and most common of venereal diseases. Early Chinese writings refer to it, and so does the Bible. The word *gonorrhea* is Greek in origin, meaning "flow of seed," and was first used by the physician Galen in 130 A. D. to describe the disease. The organism which causes it was not identified until 1839, when it was given the name "gonococcus." Like syphilis, it was not easily cured until the antibiotics appeared, and severe complications often resulted in ailments requiring specialized treatment. Now the disease is considered to be relatively minor, and its cure is usually simple if the infection is treated early enough.

Gonorrhea is almost always contracted during sexual intercourse with an infected person. The organism is ordinarily found only in the genital-urethral area, although the rectum may be infected by spreading from the genitals or from anal intercourse. It has been known to affect the skin and joints, and, much more rarely, the brain and blood system.

The first symptom of gonorrhea in a male is usually an acute urethritis, that is, an inflammation of the urethra. A thin watery discharge from the penis begins from two to seven days after an infectious sexual contact, and becomes thicker and greenish-yellow in color within another day or two. The patient usually feels an urgent and frequent need to urinate, and when he does so, there is a severe burning sensation at the tip of his penis, which now may be swollen and inflamed.

Painful complications, which are sometimes serious, frequently result from gonorrhea. One of the most agonizing is epididymitis, a condition characterized by a swelling of the epididymis, which is attached to the testicle. The testes themselves can become as large as oranges and extremely painful. Other complications may include inflammation of the eyes, skin, joints and covering of the brain.

Gonorrheal infection of the prostate can be a long and drawn-out affair, causing a male to remain infectious for a considerable length of time, and it can also produce scars that may sometimes close the urethral passage. This is a common but serious complication, which may cause the patient to develop a severe bladder or kidney disorder. Before the use of antibiotics, these complications often caused death.

One of the most distressing facts about women who are infected by gonorrhea is that about 85 percent of them have no clinical signs of the disease and therefore are not aware that they have the disease and are contagious. Thus, until the disease is diagnosed and cured they are likely to continue to infect and reinfect their sexual partners if no condom is used during sexual intercourse. If a woman does show recognizable symptoms of gonorrhea, the first sign is a vaginal discharge that begins two to seven days from the time of infectious contact. The vulva becomes red, raw and irritated. There is an urgent and frequent need to urinate, and urination itself is accompanied by pain and a scalding sensation.

Women can develop two important and distinct complications from this disease: infection of Bartholin's glands, and infection of the Fallopian tubes. These conditions frequently cause severe cramping, abdominal pain, menstrual irregularity, invalidism and sterility. Surgical treatment is often required.

Diagnosis of gonorrhea is commonly made by microscopic

examination of a smear of urethral or vaginal discharge. Treatment with antibiotics is simple and effective, but any complications resulting from the original infection will, of course, require specialized treatment. As I observed earlier, there is now at least one strain of gonococci which has developed a resistance to penicillin, and even other antibiotics, which means that a cure is a little less certain than it has been.

Syphilis and gonorrhea are the two most common venereal diseases, as I've said, but they are not the only ones. The others may not be quite as dangerous, but they are not without special perils, and because they haven't had the publicity attached to the common diseases, adolescents especially are likely to know less about recognizing them.

One of these is chancroid, a highly contagious disease spread through intercourse. The first sign appears about 12 to 16 hours after such an infectious intercourse has taken place. It usually takes the form of an inflamed eruption on the skin, ordinarily at the point of physical contact, which soon becomes a ragged-edged ulcer, filled with dead tissue. The ulcer varies in size, but it may become extremely large and destructive of the skin in the affected area. There may be only a single ulcer to begin with, but the pus oozing from it often infects the nearby areas of the body, including the man's prepuce, glans, or penile shaft. In a girl, the ulcer usually forms on the labia majora, vestibule, or clitoris. Occasionally the lymph glands of the groin may swell painfully and then rupture. If not treated, chancroid ulcerations can drain for months. Women are considerably more adversely affected by this disease than men are.

Accurate diagnosis and treatment are essential, and anyone who suspects he has this disease should see a doctor immediately so that laboratory tests can be made. Sulfonamides are the drugs most often used to treat the disease, and they usually produce a cure in from three to eight days. There are other antibiotics which are equally effective in curing chancroid quickly and permanently.

A more distinctive kind of venereal disease is granuloma inguinale. It causes widespread ulceration, and scarring of skin and the tissues beneath it. The genitals are a special area of attack, but nongenital regions are also frequently invaded. This is an infectious disease, but it is not necessarily contracted from intercourse, so "venereal" is not an entirely accurate word to describe it. It is more common in warm, tropical parts of the world than in cooler climates.

The disease begins with a small red sore, usually appearing on the penis or labia, but occasionally elsewhere—the face, neck, rectum or groin. The sores enlarge and spread, and the ulcerations grow together to form a larger area of infection. The tissue becomes a red, moist, smelly, grainy and frequently bleeding mass. Healing does not ordinarily occur without treatment, and a gradual spread of the ulceration is capable of destroying much of the tissue of the whole genital region. Normal tissue is then replaced by thick scar tissue.

In chancroid, the lymph gland is infected, but in granuloma inguinale, this is not true and the difference provides an excellent diagnostic tool to distinguish between the two diseases. The actual organism which causes the disease is hard to identify, even with a microscopic examination of tissue scraped from active ulcers. Again, antibiotic drugs, particularly those of the mycin family, are used to cure the disease.

Still another venereal disease, and another with a difficult name, is lymphogranuloma venereum. It is caused by a virus that invades the tissue in the anal-genital area. It first appears a few days after sexual contact with an infected person, and takes the form of a small blister. The blister soon ruptures to form a shallow ulcer with well-defined edges, surrounded by reddened skin. The blister is painless and heals rapidly without leaving a scar. The first sore may appear on the glans, prepuce, vulva, vaginal walls, cervix, within the urethra, or in the anal region.

About two weeks after the appearance of the first sore, the disease advances to its secondary stage, with pain in the groin followed by noticeable enlargement of the lymph glands. If the infection advances to a third stage, the symptoms become quite obvious: marked enlargement and disfigurement, known as elephantiasis, of the penis, scrotum, or vulva.

Diagnosing this disease is difficult, even in the laboratory, and antibiotic drugs have not produced the near miraculous cures in treating this virus that they have in other venereal diseases, but treatment produces at least the possibility of a cure.

Besides the venereal diseases I've just discussed, there are several other more or less common ailments affecting the reproductive organs. They may not have any relationship to sexual activity, but they may become worse if sexual contact is continued.

Probably the most common of these minor diseases is *trichomoniasis,* an annoying infection that afflicts about 25 percent of all women patients, and affects males as well, yet for some reason is seldom written about or discussed. Until recently, it was an infection that had been extremely difficult to treat.

Trichomoniasis is characterized by a discharge, itching and burning of the genitals in women; men usually don't exhibit these symptoms in any degree and most often are not aware they are infected. Trichomoniasis is caused by a tiny one-celled animal, *trichomonas vaginalis,* which is about the size and shape of a paramecium and moves in the same manner. This little body propels itself by a constant threshing of small whips at one end of its body, much like the sperm. Thousands of these organisms can be seen when a bit of infected vaginal secretion is examined under a microscope.

These trichomonads live on the surface of the vagina's membranes, rather than burrowing into the tissues. They do not invade the womb or the Fallopian tubes, but normally limit their attack to the membrane of the vagina, including the cervix. The first sign of infection is usually a white or yellowish vaginal discharge, accompanied by itching and burning. Many women find this discharge extremely worrisome because it causes constant inflammation and soreness of the external area of the vulva. When the inflamed labia are pulled apart, a thick, smelly, bubbly discharge can be seen.

To some women, trichomoniasis is not particularly irritating, but they may be annoyed by its tendency to cause severe itching. Another disadvantage is that underclothing is quickly soiled by the discharge, which gets worse before and after menstruation, as do the irritation and itching. No one knows exactly why, but some women experience severe symptoms from this infection, while others have only mild ones. Whether they are mild or severe, a doctor should be consulted immediately if the infection appears.

Men who acquire the disease usually exhibit no symptoms, although occasionally a male will experience a slight, thin, whitish discharge, or itching and burning in the urethral tract when he urinates. Anyone married or single who comes down with the infection should inform anyone he (or she, of course) may be having intercourse with, so that both can be examined, and receive treatment if necessary; otherwise one partner will simply reinfect the other. A study of married couples has shown that in 60 percent of the cases surveyed, husbands of infected wives also had the disease. The infection can be passed back and forth for many years, particularly because the males don't realize they have it. Trichomonads are found under the foreskin of uncircumcised men and in the urethral tract, and in severe cases may also invade the prostate.

It is not known exactly how this disease is contracted, other than from an infected sexual partner, but some scientists have refused to classify it as a venereal disease (and I haven't done so here) because it can be contracted in a swimming pool or a bathtub, where the organism easily finds its way into the vaginal tract.

Fortunately a new prescription drug called Flagyl has come on the market in America, and it is reported to be almost 100 percent effective in treating trichomoniasis. It is taken orally and brings about a cure within 10 to 14 days in both men and women. If a woman can't obtain this drug for any reason, some other form of medication can be applied to the vaginal area. Doctors also frequently recommend antiseptic douches. In any case, treatment needs to be carefully carried out under medical direction because, although the disease is not considered serious in the sense of endangering life, it can be extremely bothersome and certainly prevents a satisfactory sex life.

Trichomoniasis is often accompanied by other infections, and one of the most common of these is moniliasis, usually called monilia. It is a fungus infection of the genital region capable of causing acute discomfort, and is found far more often in women than among men. This organism has the power to lie inactive for long periods of time, and then to flare up when the circumstances are ripe for its growth. More frequently than not, monilia accompanies other infections, including trichomoniasis, as I've noted.

Women who suffer from this disease frequently develop white cheesy spots on the vulva, in the vagina, and on the cervix. Small ulcerations of the labia minora may also occur, and sometimes there is a thick or watery vaginal discharge. All these symptoms can lead to raw, bleeding surfaces if treatment is not prompt and careful.

Since most organisms that cause infection and irritation in the vagina thrive on menstrual blood, women afflicted with monilia often complain of the greatest discomfort and distress before, during, and immediately after menstruation.

Monilia gets around. It is sometimes found in children, and is quite likely to afflict women who have diabetes, or who have been overtreated with antibiotic vaginal suppositories which kill off the organisms that normally live in the vagina; these organisms are the natural enemy of the monilia fungus. The disease can be cured with adequate treatment by a gynecologist.

Another common illness among women is vaginitis, which means inflammation of the vaginal walls. There are several different causes including bacteria (like the organisms causing monilia and trichomoniasis), putting foreign objects into the vagina, and the use of strong chemicals. Children, and less frequently adolescents and adults, may put small objects like coins, marbles, pins, or sticks into the vagina in an attempt at masturbation, and sometimes this causes vaginitis. Douching with a chemical solution that is too strong, overmedication, and tampons inserted and then forgotten are other causes. Poor general health also lowers the body's resistance to disease, making it less resistant to low-grade infections like vaginitis. When these conditions are present, sexual intercourse may be the source of even further irritation of the vaginal tract.

Doctors sometimes resort to a vague term, "nonspecific vaginitis," as a catch-all phrase which describes perplexing problems of vaginal discharge, itching and burning which cannot be related to any particular infection. However, recent research has disclosed that the great majority of cases of vaginitis previously described as "nonspecific" are, in fact, an infection called *Haemophilus vaginalis vaginitis,* caused by bacteria that can be identified with the aid of a microscope, like the bacteria causing monilia and trichomoniasis. Doctors usually prescribe one of the mycin drugs for treatment, and they recommend that the male sexual partner be treated also, since in most cases he will have the bacteria in his urethra, usually without knowing it.

Excessive douching, or the use of too strong solutions, is the basic cause of many cases of vaginitis. Young and newly married women are too often overly concerned about feminine hygiene. Apparently they think that if a little douching is good, more must be better, and so they increase the strength and frequency. In the long run, the results can be distressing. A recent study of prison women, however, showed that daily douching with water or a mild vinegar solution did not produce the changes in the vaginal lining or any other of the ill effects claimed by some gynecologists. Apparently the real danger seems to come from douching with harsh chemicals.

Probably the best way of warding off vaginitis is to maintain good general physical health, combined with wholesome attitudes toward sex and feminine hygiene. Every woman should have a checkup by a gynecologist at least once a year, and preferably twice.

A much less common nonvenereal disease is venereal warts, which probably result from a virus infection. In a man, the warts usually appear around the base of the glans on the penis and develop quickly in the moist environment under a tight prepuce. A woman may develop venereal warts on the labia or anus, and the growths can spread to cover the entire area around them. These warts can be transmitted to other people, and to other parts of one's body. A doctor should examine them to determine the seriousness of the condition and decide what treatment is best suited to the individual case.

Skin diseases, or dermatoses, of the genital region are fairly common and are caused by a great number of organisms and substances. For example, chemicals, like those contained in soap that is not rinsed off properly after a shower, can collect in the sensitive area of the genitals and produce irritation or burns. Complications can occur if the sufferer attempts a cure with medication that is too strong for the affected area. Some people always think that if a little medicine is good, a lot will be better. They're wrong.

Boys have a common name for a common dermatosis. They called it "jock itch." Technically, it's *tinea cruris,* a disease that affects the genital region. It's a fungus and its early symptoms are reddish, scaly patches. These infected areas may become large and highly inflamed, painful and extremely itchy. "Jock itch" is much like athlete's foot. It develops as the result of sweating, tight clothing and inadequate drying of the genitals after a bath. These circumstances provide a favorable environment for the development and spreading of this fungus infection.

Equally common is the disease people call "crabs," whose technical name is *pediculosis pubis,* an itchy skin irritation caused by the tiny bites of the crab louse. Scratching causes further irritation and a brownish discoloration of the skin may develop. The crab louse usually buries its head at the root of the pubic hair and attaches its body to the hair itself. These parasites usually pass from one person to another through infectious sexual contact, although they may also be picked up from a toilet seat or a bed.

Still another annoying affliction is *pruritis,* an extreme and maddening itching, frequently in the genital-anal region. It is a common symptom of skin diseases. Medication usually provides relief from the itching, although some stubborn cases don't respond to treatment and the symptoms may continue for long periods of time.

Whenever we add "itis" to the name of an organ, it means that organ is inflamed. In this grouping are a good many disorders of the internal and external genitals that ought to be mentioned here. *Cystitis,* for example, is a not uncommon inflammation of the bladder, occurring in a variety of ways. Symptoms usually include a severe burning sensation during urination, a frequent need to urinate, and a sharp pain in the lower abdomen. Women who have it often report that the pain is especially severe if they have sexual intercourse.

When the bladder is already irritated and body resistance is low, bacteria already in the bladder or germs that enter it by way of the urethra can cause an infection. Irritation of a woman's bladder may occur as a result of frequent sexual intercourse, because of the pressure of the man's weight and the movement of the penis against her bladder and urethra through the vaginal walls. It happens so often on honeymoons that it is popularly called "honeymoon cystitis." To prevent it, a woman is wise to urinate before intercourse, and to use a lubricating jelly when nature appears not to supply enough vaginal secretion.

Cystitis can have emotional as well as physical causes. Frequently it is a result of conflict over sexual matters, and in that case, psychotherapy can be helpful in bringing about a cure. But whether the cause is emotional or physical, a doctor should be consulted at the first signs of cystitis; it is not a disease to ignore.

A fairly common sexual disorder among men is *epididymitis*, involving inflammation of the epididymis, which of course is attached to each testicle. It is in a position to become infected from the testis below, perhaps as a result of a blow to the testicle. It is also vulnerable to infection from the prostate gland or seminal vesicle above, because infection can spread to it through the vas deferens. Gonorrhea is an important cause of this disease.

This infection varies both in its length and the severity of its symptoms. In mild cases, there may be only a slight swelling and tenderness, which may respond readily to treatment. In severe cases, the entire testicle may be greatly swollen and painful. The result can be sterility, which only surgery has a chance to correct. Some cases last for years, while others respond quickly to treatment, which involves extensive use of certain drugs, a balanced and wholesome diet, rest, and a warm climate.

Older men particularly are susceptible to another disease,

prostatitis, an inflammation of the prostate gland. It often follows a lengthy period of infection in other parts of the body, but it may also be the result of unrelieved sexual tension continuing for a particularly long period of time. In the latter case, the collection of prostatic secretions causes congestion and, finally, inflammation of the prostate gland.

Symptoms of prostatitis usually include a thin mucous discharge, especially in the morning, and pain in the lower back, testicles, scrotum, and the tip of the penis. The disease may cause loss of potency, painful or inadequate erections, premature and sometimes bloody ejaculations, and sterility.

Massage of the prostate, antibiotic treatment and prolonged warm baths are the techniques used by specialists to treat this infection, and to bring about drainage of the congested gland. Even then, it is not easy to get rid of prostatitis completely.

Although it isn't a venereal disease, or even a sexual disorder, I can't leave out of this discussion something so well known as "mono," or *infectious mononucleosis,* which attacks so many adolescents and college students. It's distantly related to sexual activity through its familiar name, "the kissing disease," although that's not the only way it can be acquired. In any event, "mono" is an infectious disease of the lymph glands, and its symptoms include the sudden onset of fever, marked fatigue, chills, sweating, headache, sore throat and loss of appetite. Occasionally there are severe or (very rarely) even fatal complications, and young people who get the disease shouldn't treat it lightly because "everybody gets it."

Exactly how mono is passed from one person to another is not known definitely, but many authorities think that deep kissing with an infected person is responsible. One study found that 71 out of 73 mono patients had engaged in deep kissing with an infected person at the exact time the incubation period for mononucleosis would have begun for them. Fever usually leaves the patient after five days, and the other symptoms disappear within three weeks, although in some cases they continue for months.

7

Some physical disorders

THERE IS A WHOLE CATEGORY of sexual disorders that come under the heading of physical abnormalities of the genitals. I think they're worth talking about because knowledge of them will make you more understanding of these conditions if you encounter them in others. They are disorders caused by hereditary factors, physical complications present at birth, or else they develop after birth. There are many of them but I intend to discuss here only the most common or best known.

Ordinarily, a boy's testicles descend from his body into his scrotum at about the seventh month of the pregnancy. It has been estimated that about 1 in 50 baby boys has

99

undescended testicles at the time of birth and that about 7 percent of this affected group still have the condition at puberty. Testicles fail to descend because of such factors as inadequacy or imbalance in male hormonal secretion, or because of some blockage in the structure through which the testes must pass from the abdomen to the scrotum. Physicians generally agree that an undescended testicle should be dealt with by the time a boy is 5 or 6 years of age. Treatment with hormones will often bring about a successful descent of the testicles; otherwise surgery may be needed to make them descend into the scrotum. If they remain undescended after puberty arrives, testes will gradually waste away, and physical features like those of a castrated male will develop, especially if both testicles are involved.

More complicated and less susceptible to any kind of treatment are the disorders of the chromosomes. Normal human cells each contain 23 pairs of chromosomes, or 46 in all. One pair of these are the sex chromosomes—XX in the female and XY in the male. Recent research has shown us that some sexual disorders are related to abnormal arrangements of these chromosomes. Of these, the two best known are *Turner's syndrome* and *Klinefelter's syndrome,* named for the researchers who discovered them.

This is how Turner's syndrome comes about. Sometimes in the process of cell division during the development of human sperm and eggs, the chromosomes going into the two daughter cells split 22-24 rather than the normal 23-23. If the 22-chromosome cell should fertilize (or be fertilized), there would be only 45 chromosomes in the zygote, the fertilized egg. The result would be what is known as an XO zygote, not the normal XX or XY zygote containing 46 chromosomes. When one of the X chromosomes in the fertilized ovum is missing, the condition is called Turner's syndrome and will produce a woman with a female's external sex structure, although it will be poorly developed, and her ovaries will be completely missing.

Because ovarian hormones are lacking, the whole sexual system of these women is defective. Other signs of this syndrome are a short stature, winglike folds of skin extending from the base of the skull to an area over the shoulder bone, and a broad, stocky chest. Deafness and mental deficiency are also fairly common accompaniments.

In Klinefelter's syndrome, the zygote has an extra X chromosome, making it an XXY zygote containing 47 chromosomes rather than the normal 46. The result is a male with a distinctly female physical appearance, having testicles that are small and incapable of producing mature sperm. This is what the officials were looking for when they challenged the femaleness of some of the women entered in recent Olympic Games, and ordered them to be given blood tests which would show their chromosome count and determine whether they were really women.

New scientific instruments and research techniques are bringing us new discoveries in the structure of chromosomes. People with such abnormal arrangements as XXXY, XXXXY and XYY have been found, and the effect of these on criminal behavior is being studied.

Another abnormality, not related to chromosomes, is permanent shriveling of the testicles, far more often one than both, which is known as *atrophy,* or wasting away, *of the testicles*. This condition may exist at birth, or it may develop later as the result of an illness like mumps, or from an accident. If only one testicle is damaged, the man is still able to make a woman pregnant and his sexual ability will be quite normal in all respects.

A frequent complaint a gynecologist hears in his office concerns abnormal uterine bleeding. He terms it *"functional uterine bleeding,"* and it means a hemorrhage for which there appears to be no physical basis. Mostly it is caused by an imbalance between the hormones estrogen and progesterone, producing an unnatural growth of uterine tissue which results, in turn, in abnormal bleeding from the uterus.

I might add here that a good many people mistakenly believe that birth control pills, because they prevent ovulation, cause a disturbance of hormonal balance. This is rarely the case, and in fact the pills are often prescribed to correct just such disorders. Nevertheless, women should not have to be told to see their gynecologist regularly, particularly when there is any form of abnormal bleeding from the vagina.

Another sexual disorder is *displacement of the uterus,* in which the womb becomes fixed in an abnormal position. What is normal? When a woman is standing erect, the uterus should be about at right angles to the vagina, placing it in an almost horizontal plane above the bladder. For various reasons, the tissues that support the uterus may become too tense or too loose, and it then shifts to an unusual position. This shifting frequently causes painful menstruation, backaches, and pelvic congestion. It also makes intercourse uncomfortable. If there is no pain connected with uterine displacement, there is no need to correct the condition. It doesn't seem to interfere with the possibility of pregnancy, and properly positioning it does not seem to increase that chance.

A disorder which affects from 4 percent to 11 percent of all women is the *fibroid tumor,* incorrectly named because these tumors are formed from muscle cells, not from fibrous tissue. They occur most often among women in their fifties, although it is not uncommon for women considerably younger to develop uterine tumors of very large size. Hormonal imbalance of some sort is thought to produce fibroid tumors, since it has been shown that tumors present before the menopause either shrink or remain the same size after it. Excessive bleeding is a symptom of the disorder in about 50 percent of the cases. Treatment has to be tailored to the individual; a good gynecologist can determine what is best.

One of the most misunderstood abnormalities is *hermaphroditism.* The word is not only commonly mispronounced and misused, but a mythology has been built up around those afflicted with it. It is a condition in which an individual has the gonads of both sexes—that is, one ovary and one testicle are present. True hermaphroditism is extremely rare; there are only a few hundred true cases listed in the world's medical literature.

Technically, it would be possible for a hermaphrodite to impregnate as a male and also to conceive as a woman. A physician in Brazil recently reported a case of a true hermaphrodite who had a developing fetus in the womb, and who possessed a testicle capable of producing sperm. This patient—who could hardly be called either "he" or "she"—claimed to be both the father and the mother of the child. It may reasonably be doubted whether this was really a case of self-impregnation, because the female hormones of the ovary would certainly sterilize the testes, making the person incapable of fertilizing ova.

There is considerable variation in the number of internal and external features of both sexes in the individual hermaphrodite. Ordinarily, a hermaphrodite will grow up with the characteristics and interests of the sex assigned at birth. This shows how much stronger psychological factors are in developing "masculine" or "feminine" traits than biological factors are. Treatment includes surgical reconstruction of the genitals, along with psychotherapy if the condition is not corrected until after the second or third year of life, but each case is highly individual and has to be dealt with in the way that will best produce an emotional adjustment. Physicians now try to surgically correct the condition as soon after birth as possible.

Far more common is the disorder called *pseudohermaphroditism,* meaning false hermaphroditism. Some form of it appears in about one of every thousand infants born. In this condition, the male has gonads that are testes, at least from the standpoint of the makeup of the testicular tissues, and the gonads of the female are ovaries. The most important difference between the extremely rare hermaphrodite and the more common "pseudo" is that the former has both an ovary and a testicle, while the latter has only one kind of gonadal tissue, either testicular or ovarian. In the "psuedo," then, the kind of gonadal tissue present determines the sex of the individual, even though there are definite physical characteristics of the opposite sex.

During normal embryonic growth, the gonads develop into either testes or ovaries. In pseudohermaphrodites, however, an abnormality in cell structure occurs during early embryonic development, and either or both the gonads and the genitals, as well as the other body characteristics, take on many features of the opposite sex. These people usually have both male and female sex organs in incomplete form, and their true sex is difficult to determine.

Because the sex of the "pseudo" can be so easily misjudged, even by parents, it is not uncommon for such a child to be brought up as a member of the wrong sex. Childhood experiences quite naturally influence individuals to assume the interests, attitudes and sexual behavior of one sex, even though his body features are those of the opposite. Once a child has been reared as a certain sex for the first three or four years of his life, that child should continue to be reared as that sex no matter if the error in sex labeling is discovered. The psychological effects of being reared as one sex have already fixed that person's sex identity and to attempt a change in identity after the age of about 4 would produce far more problems than it would correct.

Finally, we come to another relative rarity, *congenital and acquired disorders of the breast*. These are found in both men and women. Among men, the most frequent is an abnormal increase in breast size. The problem may develop first during adolescence, when hormonal changes ordinarily take place, but it may also occur in adulthood as a result of newly developed hormonal disorders, or because the female hormone estrogen has been used to treat certain ailments, like cancer of the prostate. Medication to shrink the excessive breast tissue or surgery to remove it are the usual methods of treatment.

Men and women may have one or more extra breasts, extra nipples, or an abnormally enlarged breast (or breasts), or the nipple of the breast may be missing. Extra breasts and nipples usually follow the milk line, which starts under the arm, then continues through the breasts and down both sides of the abdomen in a line to the lips of the vulva, ending in the inner thighs. Plastic surgery can correct the abnormalities. While these disorders are relatively rare, as I've said, any unusual growth, pain, or changes in the feel, function, or appearance of the breast should be investigated immediately by a physician.

It's what you
believe and feel
that's important

WHAT DETERMINES PEOPLE'S attitudes toward sex? Why does one person shrink away from it, another exhibit a healthy curiosity about it, and a third embrace it as though it might go out of fashion? Out of the millions of words written on this subject, representing every conceivable point of view, it is possible to pinpoint the factors that shape our sexual attitudes, which in turn govern our sexual behavior.

Attitudes, and sex education itself, begin with the first intimate mother-infant contacts, and continue in the family relationship with whatever attitudes are communicated to the children by both parents. Never mentioning sex nor attempting to provide any

105

information about it is an attitude in itself, and has its effect. But as the child grows up, other factors outside the family circle come into play. The culture in which he lives has its general demands, and they differ from country to country, from society to society. There are also special demands and expectations based on differences in sexual morality within the culture. A variety of these pressures, then, shape our attitudes toward sex: where we live, whether we subscribe to a religious faith, whether we're male or female, how old we are, our educational level, and the socio-economic level of the individual, his parents and his teachers.

We've been hearing a great deal about the "sexual revolution" of the Sixties, but most authorities now agree that no such revolution has taken place, that it is only our attitudes and not our actual sexual behavior that has changed substantially. The last real sexual revolution occurred in the Twenties, when women born around the turn of the century came of age in a postwar world that was far different from the one they had grown up in. What has happened in America, and for that matter a good part of the Western world, in the past decade is a revolt against old attitudes toward sex and a growing freedom to talk about it, read about it, see it visually and accept it much more as a part of life instead of trying to push it under the rug.

The confusion arises—and a good many high school and college students *are* confused—from the sharp difference between our current sexual attitudes and our actual behavior. For example, in one study 75 percent of college girls believed that their classmates were "sleeping around" (an attitude), but in fact, as the study showed, only 20 percent of this group were actually experiencing premarital intercourse (a matter of behavior).

Major changes in moral codes, behavior, laws and social institutions occur gradually, and people in every country are inclined to cling to their traditional ways of thinking and behaving. This is particularly true of Americans where sex is concerned. They are reluctant to accept change or be swayed by outside influences. I can understand why adolescents are particularly impatient with their parents' rigid attitudes toward sex, but they might remember that their fathers and mothers had their attitudes shaped by *their* parents. When today's adolescents are parents of teenagers, they in turn will be confronted by a new generation who think they're old-fashioned.

Cultural differences produce a wide variety of sexual attitudes. Sometimes they're so different between cultures and within the same culture that sexual behavior considered normal and natural in one place may be condemned as abnormal or absurd in another. Adolescents who spend their summers traveling in Europe and other parts of the globe are especially conscious of these differences. They discover, for example, that the strong disapproval of premarital and extramarital activity which is so evident among older Americans is not shared by the majority of the world's cultures. One study of 158 societies throughout the world showed that 70 percent of them don't condemn premarital intercourse, although they don't go so far as to accept adulterous relationships freely.

Examples of differences in our own culture are numerous. A college-educated man who is taking a survey of the sexual habits of Americans, for instance, will interview and record the histories of people with much less education. Unless he has been adequately prepared for it, he will be astounded when he hears about some of the sexual experiences of people who live on a different level than his own. On the other hand, one of the interviewees, with only a grade school education, or less, is likely to think the oral-genital behavior of a college-educated couple, if he hears about it, is perverted and totally objectionable.

Investigations by anthropologists tell us that cultures which encourage women to be completely free in their sexual expression produce females whose sexual response is as uninhibited and vigorous as that of their men. Cultures that approve of women having orgasms produce orgasmic women, and cultures that don't approve, produce women who are incapable of orgasms.

Misinformation and prudery affect sexual attitudes profoundly. Women in modern societies are frequently troubled with menstrual difficulties, for instance, but the anthropologist Margaret Mead found that among the women of the South

Pacific island of Samoa, only one woman of the entire population even understood what was meant by pain or emotional upset during menstruation. That one woman worked for the island's only white missionary family!

The Women's Liberation movement so much discussed now, which had its real beginnings in the struggle for equal voting rights at the beginning of the century and before, has resulted in what may be the greatest social change of our century. The freedom and equal rights that women now demand and to some extent enjoy in America have had a marked effect on present-day sexual attitudes, and possibly may have an even greater effect in the future. Large segments of American women have grown away from the Victorian viewpoints that dominated life in this country for so long, and they understand how wrong the old ideas were. In matters of sex, for instance, most no longer believe that men and women have basically different sexual needs and drives, that women should have little interest in sex, and that they take part in sexual activity only to have children or please the husband. Now they realize that they have as much right as men to expect sexual gratification in marriage.

A side effect has been that the sexual attitudes of American women are often considerably healthier than those of the men. Researchers who take sexual histories report that women are far more open and honest in supplying information about their intimate personal lives than men. The men frequently get tangled up in the problem of self-esteem, and try to offset what they feel is a threat to their self-image by boasting of sexual exploits.

But in spite of what women have achieved in the struggle for their rights there remain some differences in the sexual attitudes.of men and women. They are accounted for by the way the two sexes are brought up, by what society expects from them, and by certain physiological factors. No matter how much the "new freedom" is advertised, for example, premarital chastity for girls is still considered the norm by much of American society, even though most people no longer believe that all premarital intercourse is evil and that offenders should be punished. Religious and moral codes condemn such intercourse, family training is aimed against it, fears are carefully cultivated and the idea that it is best to wait until marriage is an article of faith among older people especially. Lack of opportunity inhibits premarital sex in some cases, and in a few others there is lack of desire. Before the Pill, fear of pregnancy was sometimes a controlling factor, but the ability to obtain this and other contraceptives has pretty well removed that inhibition. It should be noted, however, that Kinsey found in the Fifties that one-half of all married American women had had premarital sexual intercourse. Also, the latest surveys indicate that there has not been a great increase in the frequency of premarital intercourse among married American women, although there has been some. The Pill has not, therefore, been a significant factor in increasing the amount of premarital intercourse in the United States. It has simply removed the fear of pregnancy for many girls.

Other major factors have been operating in this country to change sexual attitudes. One is the overlong period of adolescence enforced on American youth by demands for additional educational and vocational training. At the same time, the age of physical maturity comes considerably earlier than it did for previous generations. Consequently, the period of what we might call "social adolescence" is now about twice as long as it was a hundred years ago.

During this extended period, the two sexes begin to develop different attitudes toward premarital sexual activity. Natural feelings of insecurity in adolescence, plus the increase in sexual drive, especially in boys, make teenagers easy victims for the kind of advertising that places high value on sex appeal as a means of gaining popularity, success, admiration and security. Boys are led to believe that their masculinity depends upon their success in seduction; the further they can go, the more masculine they are in their own eyes and those of their friends.

On the other hand, girls are taught the importance of being sexy. They are encouraged on every hand to buy products advertised as guaranteed to increase sexual attractiveness. That puts a young girl in a difficult position. She has to appear and act sexy so she can attract as many boys and have as many dates as possible, because these are the symbols of popularity and social success. At the same time, she must control her sexual behavior; otherwise she risks losing her "good girl" status. Teenagers don't seem to recognize any in-between: either she does or she doesn't; she's a good girl or a pushover. Friends measure her by her popularity in dating—and by her ability to stay out of sexual involvements.

Teenage girls have their own particular anxieties, too. They are often concerned over the shape and size of their breasts, much as boys are over the size of their penis, especially since the breasts are so much more visible. Small breasts become a symbol of inferiority for many girls, a fact that has made a great deal of money for brassiere-padding businesses, who have deliberately encouraged it. Typical is the shop that advertises: "We fix flats!" Plastic surgeons have been called upon to develop ingenious methods for remolding breasts into desired shapes and sizes through surgery and plastics, some of them dangerous. Visiting foreigners often remark on the American preoccupation with breasts, reflected in advertising and clothing styles alike. Even toy stores go along with this preoccupation by keeping their shelves well stocked with high-bosomed dolls.

If girls (and men too) were more familiar with history and the rest of the world, they would know that breast appeal varies from culture to culture and from era to era, and that breast size and shape have nothing to do with sexuality, except psychologically. About 75 percent of men are sexually excited by stimulating a woman's breast, but only about 50 percent of women consider this kind of sex play exciting.

I should add that both male and female breasts have many nerve endings which produce sexual excitement and pleasure when properly stimulated (some women can even come to orgasm this way), but the point is that there are no more of these endings in large breasts than in small ones. As far as breastfeeding is concerned, large breasts are not necessarily an advantage because they often contain an excessive amount of fat tissue that can interfere with the function of the milk glands.

The development of breasts in a woman with normal hormone output is mostly a matter of heredity, and nothing much can be done with exercise, injection of hormones, or the application of creams and salves to alter nature's original design. If women understood that, the makers of various worthless and often expensive preparations and mechanical devices would have to go out of business. Sagging breasts can be prevented to some degree by well-designed and properly fitted brassieres, but a good posture, sensible diet and proper hygiene remain the greatest assets for an attractive figure. A physician can provide the best advice for preventing the breakdown of breast tissue during pregnancy, breastfeeding and weaning. If a woman finds the size and shape of her breasts unsatisfactory, the use of a padded and properly supportive brassiere is the most sensible solution.

There is another danger in the overevaluation of breasts as symbols of femininity. Women caught up with this idea often avoid proper physical examinations for fear that some previously unnoticed abnormality of the breast will be discovered, and that surgery will be needed, thus destroying their femininity. This refusal to face the possibility of breast cancer creates a needless danger to the lives of many women.

Younger teenagers accept with little questioning the sexual teachings of their parents—up to a point. But as they pass that point and grow a little older, they begin to think more and more independently and come under the influence of values outside the family, particularly the ones held by their friends.

Girls break away from the past and from their families less than boys, in spite of all we hear and read. Slightly more than half of teenage girls admit to guilt feelings if they go "too far" in petting with their dates, while only a quarter of the boys express similar guilt. There are other differences. Boys are more interested in petting and sexual intercourse, while the girls are willing to neck—an old word, meaning mild embracing and kissing limited to face and lips—but they want to stop there. As a relationship becomes more serious, progressing from dating to going steady, and then to engagement, sexual behavior naturally becomes more intimate, but guilt over sexual expression becomes less strong in both sexes.

Study after study has told us about the marked difference between what parents themselves have experienced (or are experiencing) in terms of sexual activity, and what they teach their children about proper sexual behavior. Mothers who have had premarital intercourse aren't sorry and say they would do it again, but they illogically expect their daughters to exert greater control over their behavior than they did. The reason for this paradox is complex but it comes down to responsibility. Studies have shown that a married couple with no children have a more liberal attitude toward premarital sexual intercourse than couples with very young children, who, in turn, have a more liberal attitude than those parents who have teen-aged children, especially daughters. Older brothers and sisters may have a quite liberal view toward premarital sex during their own teenage and early adult life, but if they have younger sisters approaching those years when one is tempted to try premarital intercourse, they quickly develop quite conservative views insofar as their younger sisters are concerned. The parents and older brothers and sisters feel responsible for the youths and develop attitudes and behavior that are designed to protect them. Parents are more conservative regarding premarital sexual acts for their daughters than they are for their sons. Interestingly, when the youths who are tempted to engage in premarital sex become parents with their own teenagers and young unmarried adults, they will become about as conservative in these matters as their parents were.

For a man, love usually follows a sexual attraction, but for a woman, sexual involvement usually follows romantic attachment. That is the fundamental difference. As a rule, a girl has to have a strong emotional attachment before she permits herself to be sexually involved. She has to be convinced that it's she, as a person, who is important to the relationship, not just her sexuality. Girls enter college, for example, with conservative sexual attitudes, then shift later in their academic lives to more liberal standards—but *only* if they become engaged, in most cases. The change appears to be the result of their growing emotional involvement and commitment, ending in the engagement. Within a few years after finishing college, and after marriage, these women then tend to return to their conservative pre-engagement attitudes concerning premarital sexual behavior.

In her own premarital sexual experiences, a mother may have had strong feelings for the man with whom she was sexually involved, but somehow she can't accept the fact that her daughter may be just as mature as she was at the time of her premarital intercourse. She finds it hard to accept that her daughter may also recognize the importance of being emotionally involved before she is sexually involved. Mothers simply can't identify strongly enough with daughters to appreciate the depth of a girl's feelings when she becomes emotionally attached to a young man. Neither can she accept the fact that the involvement may have permitted the daughter to develop a liberal sexual viewpoint of her own.

A further complication is the fact that the mother may still have a considerable amount of guilt feelings about her own early behavior because she acted against the sexual code under which *her* mother brought her up. Her feelings of guilt may break through and be projected onto her maturing daughter. As a result, the mother disapproves of *any* premarital sexual experience on the daughter's part.

Another example of the curious differences between attitude and behavior in our society lies in the fact that many people, especially men, find it hard to enter into a warm, close, loving relationship with others. Little boys are often taught that to be tender and have warm feelings for others is to be a sissy. Little girls are taught that to be warmly responsive is to run the risk of being considered aggressive.

To grow up in an environment that places heavy controls on positive emotional responses makes it likely that people will learn to express only negative emotions, like anger and hostility. But these people grow into adulthood with the understanding that some warm emotional exchanges are important and expected in successful relationships. Since they learned in their early years to express only negative emotional responses, these people actually start quarrels or fights with their sexual partners to express the only kind of emotion they really understand. Men who have never learned how to express tenderness, or who are afraid to do so, will often ignore the woman with whom they are sexually involved, or make belittling remarks to her. These men *want* to show their true feelings, but since they don't know how to express positive emotions, they use the only emotional expressions they are familiar with—the negative ones.

In the same way that many adults are inclined to divide women into "princesses" or "prostitutes," figuratively speaking, some teenage boys take the attitude that "good girls don't, bad girls do," which causes them to seek intercourse with girls they don't care for because they consider girls they respect as being "too good" to be involved in sexual activity. Because of their fondness for the "good girls," however, and their emotional closeness to them, the boys may become sexually aroused. As this relationship gets closer and deeper, the couple's behavior may well lead to intercourse, and then the boy often loses respect for the "good girl," who in his eyes has now turned "bad," and he may quite likely end the relationship—or develop strong guilt feelings for seducing a "good girl."

Over a period of time, patterns in guilt feelings undergo a change in both sexes, especially among older unmarried people. Therapists report that many men have considerably more guilt over sexual matters than women. Women, especially in premarital sex relationships, usually and understandably want to be certain they are desired for something more than just sex. They also want assurance that the men with whom they have intercourse won't "kiss and tell," and will still have the same respect for them after the sexual act. On the other hand, a man feels that he is the "seducer" in this act, and so the responsibility for the girl's part in it rests on his shoulders. To calm his own guilt or anxiety, consequently, he must feel either that there is love in the relationship, or that the girl is "bad." Since he feels guilty about his "seduction" of the girl, he comes to view her as the cause of his guilt and becomes angry with her. Then he expresses his anger by quarreling or fighting with her, belittling her, or otherwise showing his rejection of her—and this is the same girl who thought enough of him to share the most personal of human experiences.

Since girls are less likely than boys to be sexually involved if they're not emotionally involved, they frequently develop guilt feelings if their sexual activities are not accompanied by love on their part. The common danger here is that if a girl is only sexually attracted to a boy, and if she can't accept these physical desires for what they are, she might well imagine herself to be in love in order to make her desires acceptable. Marriage, and even a child, may follow, but after sexual desire (or maybe it's only curiosity) is satisfied, she wakes up to the realization that not only was she not in love, but the physical attraction is gone as well. Boys are not immune to this kind of self-deception, of course. It's hard to say this to teenagers, because it's so hard to believe it when you're young, but the most mature thing they can do is to learn to distinguish between what is merely romantic delusion or sexual attraction and what is genuine love, based on a good many other things.

For married people, this kind of thinking quite often leads to extramarital relationships. Bored with an unexciting but devoted husband or wife, one partner finds himself, or herself, carried away by a handsome set of muscles or a well-filled bikini. Each partner may see the other realistically, but each sees the new romantic interest only in the light of physical attractiveness. Confusing sexual desire with love may lead to divorce and a new marriage—only to discover that the second time around can be just as unexciting as the first.

When extramarital affairs occur, the difference in attitudes between men and women crops up again. Men are considerably more upset by the wives' affairs than women are by the husbands'. Only 27 percent of all women would consider their husband's adultery sufficient grounds for divorce, but 51 percent of the men would regard a wife's unfaithfulness as totally destructive of the marriage. This is a part of the double standard which has so complicated our sexual relationships.

Women are not likely to demand virginity in their husbands at the time of marriage but men often expect their brides to be virgins—about 20 percent as compared with 40 percent. More highly educated men are less disturbed today than their counterparts were in the past if their bride is not virginal, but they still *prefer* that she have no previous sexual experience. Women, surprisingly, accept the male idea that sexual conquests and experience are indications of masculinity, so they often prefer that the man be sexually experienced at the time of marriage.

In their midteens, girls begin to recognize that in our society the male is supposed to be strong and confident, and to offer security to his female. Whether or not she has been indoctrinated with the idea of female inferiority, she will look for genuine strength in a boy. Without experience or adequate training, however, a girl really doesn't know what to look for as indications of masculine strength. And not knowing, she may turn to something obvious, like the hell-raiser who defies all rules of society and society itself, the leather-jacketed thug on a motorcycle, the school dropout committed to alcohol or drugs, or the dragster who is contemptuous alike of human life and human feelings.

Girls who accept these lifestyles as evidence of strength don't have the psychological insight to see that these boys are attempting to cover up their own feelings of inferiority. Consequently a girl may invite the very things she wanted to avoid, inadequacy and weakness in a man. Unfortunately, a boy who tries to treat a girl with honesty and consideration and has no need to prove his adequacy by "tough guy" behavior may be ignored or regarded with contempt.

Other factors enter into the complex emotional makeup of these girls. As they reach a new level of physical maturity, they feel inadequate to cope with the new social and sexual problems it brings. Since they think of themselves as being rather worthless and insufficient, they may twist the meaning of a boy's actions. If a boy behaves decently and kindly toward them they may reason, more or less subconsciously, that he can't have very good judgment if he offers his friendship so unselfishly. The girls therefore conclude that a boy who treats them with respect must not be of much value himself!

Having arrived at that point, the reasoning goes on to its inevitable conclusion. Boys who unfeelingly ignore or mistreat them must be showing *good* judgment, and obviously must be the strong, masculine ones, desirable both socially and sexually. To add to the confusion, girls of this age have normal sexual desires and wishes, but they frequently feel guilty about them, and the conventional reasoning is that guilt demands punishment. By selecting a "tough guy," a girl is able not only to satisfy her sexual desires but at the same time to assure her punishment, because she knows in her heart that sooner or later she will be mistreated or rejected by him. Carried over into adult life, this unconscious need to be punished explains why many women marry "problem" men—alcoholics, for example.

Personality, as well as emotions, plays an important role in creating sexual attitudes. A psychologist who has studied this problem divided women into three groups: high-dominance, low-dominance, and middle-dominance. Women rating high in dominance feelings—high self-esteem, that is—are self-confident and self-assured. They display feelings of superiority with little evidence of shyness or self-consciousness. Women with low self-esteem show just the opposite personality traits, while the middle-dominance women feel about midway between these extremes.

All this seems self-evident, but since dominance traits affect behavior as well as attitudes, it is not hard to distinguish behavior patterns forming around these groups. High-dominance women, for instance, are much more likely than those in the low-dominance group to masturbate, to have premarital sexual intercourse, to volunteer for sex research studies, and to make no effort to avoid pelvic examinations. They are generally less hesitant or embarrassed in all sexual matters.

A contradiction is that Jewish women are generally higher in both dominance feelings and dominance behavior than Catholic or Protestant women, but they have a higher percentage of virginity than either of the other two religious groups. Women who are strongly religious, no matter what their faith, are more likely to be virgins, not to masturbate, and in general to react less positively to sexual matters than women with less devout religious feelings.

The most satisfactory marriages are those in which the husband equals his wife in dominance feelings, or else is somewhat (but not greatly) superior to her in this respect. If a wife has higher dominance feelings than the husband, however, or if he is significantly more dominant than she is, the result is likely to be poor social and sexual adjustment, unless they're both very secure people.

Apparently like attracts like. High-dominance women are attracted only to high-dominance men, and they want them to be straightforward, passionate, and a little violent in their lovemaking. They want them to get on with intercourse quickly, and not spend a long time in foreplay. By contrast, the middle-dominance woman prefers gentle and prolonged wooing, with sex only a part of an atmosphere that includes loving words, tenderness, soft music and low lights. High-dominance women unconsciously want to be overpowered, while the middle-dominance woman wants to be gently seduced. The low-dominance woman simply wishes to be left alone.

When high-dominance people marry, they are likely to experiment with almost every form of sexual activity known to sexologists, including some that would be considered abnormal by low-dominance people.

From this study, which I think accurately reflects the sexual situation, it is obvious how important emotions and personality factors are in arriving at both sexual and marital adjustment.

Women often accuse their husbands of showing affection toward them only when they want to have intercourse. Husbands deny it. What happens is that the husband wants to show affection toward his wife and has no other motive, but in the process of expressing it, if his wife responds warmly, he may become sexually excited. Then she accuses him of showing affection only because he wants sex, which was not the initial intent of the husband at all.

Fortunately men and women can be taught to permit themselves the joy of experiencing close, understanding, warm and loving relationships. If they don't learn through the normal growing up process, or from experience and observation, psychotherapy can help them understand the great value of open affection. When they recognize that the free expression of affection is nothing to fear, and is not a sign of weakness, all their human relationships, including the sexual one, will be much fuller and happier.

Teenagers could save themselves a lot of grief and misery,

both as adolescents and adults, if they could realize that so many of our sexual hangups are the result of a failure to understand the people we love the most. And if we don't understand *them,* it isn't surprising that we don't understand those we don't know well. Maybe the worst mistake we make is in refusing even to *try* to understand people we think of as "different." We're suspicious of them because their skin color is different, or they live in some other place, or their religion is different, or their politics, or their clothes are not like ours.

It shouldn't be necessary to say so, but unfortunately it is: We would all be better off if we lived with an attitude of understanding and tolerance toward everyone, including those who are not like us. This is especially true in sexual behavior, one of the most sensitive areas of human differences. I've tried to show in this chapter some of the forces that make us think the way we do about sexual matters. In the following one, we'll examine the effects of these attitudes on sexual behavior, in the hope that you will better understand and accept what people do about sex—even when their behavior isn't what you would choose for yourself, or what conventional society prescribes for us.

9

How people express their sex drive

"HUMAN" SEXUAL BEHAVIOR, we say. And that's where the trouble begins. A few years ago two Yale scientists compared forty animal and human societies and showed us that patterns of sexual behavior were the same in all of them. We don't do anything that animals don't do, or vice versa. The big difference is that humans are profoundly influenced by strong psychological, social and cultural pressures that transform the simple biological patterns common to all forms of life into something else. That "something else" is so complex that a web of ignorance, distortion and outright dishonesty has grown up about human sexual behavior, which makes it difficult to measure or even to understand our experiences.

Because sexual activity is such a fundamental and joyous experience, it is strange that only in the sexual area, among all the areas of human existence, have guilt, confusion and emotional problems managed to influence us in such a damaging way. Ignorance seems to be the chief villain here. Teenagers (and a great many adults as well) simply don't have enough accurate information about the different forms of human sexual behavior, how many people are involved in these forms, and how often they occur. That may sound dry and statistical, like "taking the fun out of sex," but only if we understand what people actually do about sex, and in what numbers, can we begin to accept the whole broad and complex pattern of human sexuality. Moreover, having the facts drains off the tension caused by unsatisfied curiosity, and if a teenager has made what he thinks is a sexual error in his life, he can see that others have made it too—and maybe it wasn't a mistake after all, but simply a variation in behavior. "I thought I was the only one who did that!" How often a therapist hears this surprised response when a patient discovers that just about everyone does or has done the same thing.

Let's begin with the sex drive itself. Basically, it is equal in males and females, as we've seen, but, generally speaking, each sex responds differently to psychological and physiological stimulation. As a group, men respond far more easily to psychological stimuli—erotic sights or sounds, exotic scents, sexy movies or books. Women respond to such stimulation, too, in widely varying ways, but as a group they are much more easily aroused by physical stimulation and romantic involvements.

The myth that women are sexually less responsive than men seems to be slowly disappearing these days, but it's easy to see how it was perpetuated so long when we think that for generations women have been conditioned to restrict or deny their sexuality altogether, and to hold back their normal responses to sexual stimuli. These restrictions and a fear of pregnancy have conveyed a completely mistaken idea about their responsiveness.

Individual response to particular forms of sexual stimulation varies greatly, as it does in all kinds of human behavior. But in spite of the basic differences between men and women in what stimulates them sexually and how they respond to it, there is probably more similarity between the sexes in their responses than there is among members of the same sex.

People often think of sexual expression as taking only one form, intercourse between a man and woman—and a good many think there is only one form of *that,* with the man above and the woman below, and everything else a perversion. In reality, intercourse is only one form of expression. There are five other ways: Masturbation, nocturnal orgasm, heterosexual petting, homosexual relations, and sexual contact with animals.

I'm going to be talking in this chapter about people according to levels of education, and so I had better define my terms. Grade school, or the low educational group, means 8 years of schooling or less; high school, the middle educational group, means 9 to 12 years; and college, the high educational group, 13 or more years. Similarly, I'll be talking about "incidence" and "frequency" in specific sexual patterns of behavior. "Incidence" refers to the number of individuals in the population who have experienced a particular form of behavior, whether once or a thousand times. "Frequency" refers to the number of times a particular form of behavior has been engaged in by the same person, or by a percentage of the population.

With all this understood, then, let's consider the five other ways of sexual expression besides intercourse, beginning with masturbation (also called "jack off" or "jerk off"). This is a term that applies to any form of stimulation of one's own self that produces sexual arousal or release. It is a common practice among males and females before, during and after marriage.

For many years children were brought up to believe that it was abnormal, and therefore wrong. Now we know that only under extremely rare circumstances can it be considered abnormal. If it were, most of us would be emotionally disturbed, since well over 95 percent of men and 70 percent of women practice it at one time or another in their lives. Only when a person uses masturbation as his sole and preferred means of sexual outlet, although other outlets are readily available, can it justifiably be considered as abnormal.

Also, only in cases where masturbation is done publicly and

compulsively as in the case of some severely disturbed mental patients is there a possibility that masturbation can be carried to extremes—another myth of the past. Nature carefully regulates our sexual activity, and when any form of it is overdone, it is no longer pleasant or desirable and the individual avoids it. Sometimes you will hear it said that someone with an emotional problem has caused it by masturbating. Older people sometimes try to prevent youngsters from masturbating by telling them that it will cause insanity ("it will make you go crazy!"). That is both unrealistic and unscientific. It is safe to say that the only emotional problems produced by masturbation in teenagers come from parents, teachers, or other boys and girls who pass on their own disturbed attitudes toward a perfectly normal act. Any act has to be considered normal if so overwhelming a proportion of the population engages in it, especially, when the act, like masturbation, is only beneficial and not at all harmful.

On the other hand, both boys and girls can acquire real anxieties and guilt feelings about masturbation because of the attitudes they've been taught, and in that case it is only sensible to stop until the psychological problem behind these feelings is corrected. This is true of all normal behavior, of course. If a person becomes conditioned to believe that drinking water is shameful and harmful, then he should stick to fruit juice when he's thirsty and get professional help for his problem.

Almost all males have masturbated or will do so, as the statistics show, although college and high school males are more likely to masturbate than the less educated. Boys usually masturbate two or three times a week, but a much higher frequency—even several times a day—is not unusual and is well within the range of normality. The act is usually accompanied by fantasies and a boy shouldn't be ashamed or disturbed if these fantasies are wild; they are only fantasies and have little or nothing to do with his real life.

In females, the higher the education level the more likely masturbation is to occur, just as it is in males. Regardless of their age or marital status, women masturbate about once every two to four weeks, although again there is the widest possible variation, from only a few times in a lifetime to several times a day. People of both sexes who have very strong religious beliefs are less likely to masturbate, and when they do, quite naturally will have more feelings of guilt and anxiety about it.

Parents who want their children—both boys and girls—to have a healthy and normal sex life should discuss masturbation with them and encourage them to use it as a normal, beneficial method of sex release when it is needed. However, not many parents can do this because of their own hangups over masturbation or because they simply do not think the problem through.

Another form of sexual expression, an involuntary one, is the nocturnal orgasm, or "wet dream," as it is so often called. For a long time it was widely believed that only males have nocturnal orgasms. This was because the evidence of boys or men having ejaculated while they were asleep was easily seen on their stained sheets. But women have erotic dreams too, as we know now, and frequently they also result in orgasms. For both men and women, however, sexual dreams often have an aggravating way of stopping just short of orgasm.

Almost all men have nocturnal dreams ending in orgasm, especially when more direct methods of sexual expression have not been used recently for some reason. The incidence is considerably higher among college men than among the less educated, perhaps because college men do more petting that is not followed by orgasm, so their sexual tensions are more frequently at a high pitch when they go to bed, and find release in the wet dreams.

About three-fourths of all women have had dreams with a sexual content, but only about half of them have had dreams ending in orgasm. Another difference is that in men the highest incidence occurs among younger males, while in women it is highest among females in their forties. Still another difference is that in men there is little relationship between the strength or weakness of their religious convictions and whether they have wet dreams, but in women, the devout have fewer nocturnal orgasms than the others.

So far we've been talking about things people do to *themselves* sexually. When it comes to what we do with other people, there's no better place to begin than the kind of activity familiar to nearly every teenager. Whatever *you* may call it, the psychologist knows it as heterosexual petting.

This kind of outlet involves conscious, sexually directed physical contact between people of opposite sex. Petting stops short of actual intercourse, but it includes a range of activities from simple kissing to genital contact. We think of petting as something only humans do, but many animals do it too in varying ways, both before and after intercourse. In marriage, petting is assumed to be a foreplay to actual intercourse; sometimes, however, for one reason or another, it is chosen in preference to intercourse as a means of reaching orgasm.

As you might expect, the incidence of petting among young men increases according to age. By 25, about 9 out of 10 men have done some petting, and about a third of them have petted to orgasm. But the lower the education level, the less likely it is that a man will pet.

Almost all women engage in petting at one time or another. The more advanced a girl's level of education, the more liberal she is likely to be in the kinds of petting she practices. Petting to orgasm consistently provides for women of all ages a higher percentage of total sexual outlet than it does for men, although both sexes average about five or six orgasmic responses per year through petting. For some individuals, however, the normal frequency may be as high as seven to ten times per week. And once again, the stronger the religious conviction, the more controlled the petting behavior, especially among women.

Sexual expression isn't always directed toward the opposite sex. Sometimes it goes toward someone of the same sex, and then we call it homosexuality. Like so many other forms of expression, this one has been considerably liberated by the greater sexual freedom of our time. Once it was hardly discussed in polite society, which condemned it in all its forms. Now it has been the subject of several Broadway plays and the topic appears often in motion pictures. It is also the frequent subject of books and magazine articles, and is discussed freely in newspapers, where it was once never mentioned except by indirection.

Opposition to it in our culture, both legal and social, has always been stronger for men than for women, but now homosexuals of both sexes have united to obtain recognition of their legal rights by the courts and to fight for their acceptance as a part of society. Homosexuality is not confined to humans; it occurs in many species of male and female animals, from cats and dogs to the wildest of wild species. It appears in birds and insects as well.

One of Dr. Kinsey's most useful contributions was his scale of human sexual behavior, with total heterosexuality at one end, and total homosexuality at the other. Relatively few people belong at either extreme. As Kinsey demonstrated, most people fall close to the middle of the scale, which has ratings from 0 to 6. This means that at some period in their lives a great many people have had at least one homosexual experience, and whether they have had more than one determines where they belong on the scale—at 1, 2, 3, 4 or 5, but seldom at 0 or 6.

In general, sexologists accept that about 4 percent of all white men are exclusively homosexual all their sexual lives, and 8 percent are exclusively homosexual for at least two years of their lives; 37 percent experience at least some form of homosexual contact to the point of orgasm. While these percentages apply only to white men, it has been estimated that they apply equally to black men.

There seems to be little relationship between educational achievement and the incidence of homosexuality among single men, but there is considerable difference in the percentage of total sexual outlet that their homosexual practices represent. The high school group has almost twice as much of its sexual outlet through homosexual contact as the grade school group does, and about four times more than the college group.

The incidence of homosexuality among women is only about one-third to one-half as much as that among men. Although no one has offered a satisfactory explanation for the difference, there is reason to believe that the statistics are influenced by the fact that homosexual contacts are much more common among preadolescent boys than girls. In contrast to other forms of sexual outlet, there is apparently no increase in female homosexuality (more familiarly called lesbianism) among women born after 1900 than among those born earlier.

Some investigations have shown us that fully half of the female population have experienced "intense feelings" for another woman, or women, during their sexual lives. Most sexologists say that about 28 percent of women, as compared with 50 percent of men, have experienced some sort of homosexual response, and that about 13 percent of women, as compared with 37 percent of men, have experienced orgasm through homosexual contact. More recent studies lead us to believe that the figures may well be higher. In fact, the higher the level of educational achievement for women, the greater is the incidence of homosexual contact, and as might be expected, among both women and men, the more devout an individual's religious beliefs are, the less homosexual contact to the point of orgasm.

To many people (although, judging from the statistics, not as many as one might believe) homosexual contact is a disgusting, or at least a distasteful, idea. Even more so is the idea of having sexual contact with animals. This is reinforced by the taboos established in the Old Testament and the Talmud, which of course would not have been so vehement about it if the practice had not existed since early civilization. Bestiality, as it is called, is not frequently practiced and has little importance as a sex outlet. Consequently, the small incidence of this sex activity is not significant in itself, but it is worth mentioning because of society's curiosity and negative reaction about it.

Not surprisingly, male contact with animals occurs primarily among boys reared on farms. About half of all farm boys have had some form of sexual contact with animals, although not many of them have carried it to the point of orgasm. Very few females have any sort of sexual contact with animals, whether on the farm or not, as far as one can judge from available studies, which may not be entirely reliable in this particular respect. When such contact does take place, it often occurs during the years before adolescence.

I've been discussing five different forms of sexual outlet, but I think it's safe to say that the sixth kind, heterosexual intercourse, outstrips all the others in popularity—and no pun intended. Other outlets may be important to people in various ways, and at different times, but intercourse between males and females is a vital part of relationships between men and women. It occurs before marriage, it happens outside marriage, and it continues after death, divorce or legal separation end a marriage.

Let's begin at the beginning of those situations with premarital intercourse. This term is often used loosely and inaccurately, but it means that at least one of the partners is single and has not been previously married. In our society, however, it has come to imply that two single persons are involved.

As everyone knows, American culture gives men considerably more freedom of sexual expression than women, and the double standard is more prevalent in premarital intercourse than in any other kind of sexual activity.

Where men are concerned, the statistics are enlightening. At some time before they're married, 98 percent of men who have attended grade school, 84 percent of those who went to high school, and 67 percent of those who got to college will have intercourse. Moreover, the incidence is about seven times greater among young men of ages 16 to 20 of grade school level than among those of the same age who are either in college or intend to go to college. Incidence among the high school group stands about midway between the other two. Males at grade-school level are most likely to have their experience with prostitutes, while those at college level are the least likely to do so.

Frequency of premarital intercourse among men is extremely varied. It ranges from a single contact during a lifetime to as many as 25 or more contacts a week, a pattern that may continue as long as five years or more. At the upper end of the social-educational scale, many men limit their premarital intercourse to one girl, and it is often the one they eventually marry. At the lower end of this scale, men may have intercourse with as many as several hundred girls.

A few single men have intercourse with older women (single, married or divorced), but nearly all the sexual experiences of these men are with single women, usually their own age or slightly younger. There are some class differences. Boys at a higher social level may take sexual advantage of girls at a lower level although this is less true now than it used to be. Young people in college almost always have their sexual experiences with persons of the same class.

Millions of Americans were shocked and outraged when in 1953, Dr. Kinsey disclosed that nearly 50 percent of all women had experienced intercourse before marriage. If they had read beyond the headlines, and looked at the Report itself, they would have discovered that about half the single women who had such intercourse engaged in it only with the men they eventually married, and that most of it took place only during the year or two just before marriage. That was the situation in the Forties and Fifties, at least; whether these figures would hold up in the Seventies, with the revolutionary Sixties intervening, no one knows, although available evidence does show the incidence to be somewhat higher today. Except for girls who married quite young, premarital intercourse during the early teens was relatively rare at the time of Kinsey's study, although this too seems to have changed some in the last two decades.

Age at the time of marriage is a significant factor in the incidence of premarital intercourse at different educational levels. Sixty percent of the girls who have gone to college, and about half the girls who finished high school have premarital intercourse, while only about a third of girls who haven't gone beyond grade school do so. But these statistics are somewhat misleading. Girls of lower education tend to marry considerably earlier, and obviously they have fewer pre-marriage years to form attachments leading to intercourse. It's interesting to note that after 20, among all women, no matter what their educational background, the incidence of premarital intercourse is about equal. Whatever the age or education, about half the women who have premarital intercourse limit their activity to a single partner whom they eventually marry.

In spite of the careful watch so many parents keep over their adolescent children, more than half the girls involved in premarital intercourse have it at least some of the time in their parents' home. Love—and sex—will find a way, apparently.

Parents should remember that even closely watched Juliet was able to entertain Romeo in her bedroom.

For both sexes and at all social-educational levels, religion is directly related to premarital sexual activity, and as one might expect, the more devout the individual, the less likely he is to engage in it.

I don't suppose any sexual subject has been argued more fiercely or at more length in America than premarital intercourse. Enough has been written about it to fill a small library, and I'm not going to repeat what is so familiar. But it may be worthwhile to summarize the arguments, pro and con, and then I'll tell you what *I* think about the subject.

Here are the arguments *for* premarital intercourse:

1. An individual's sex drive may be so strong it can only be satisfied through intercourse.
2. It gives you great physical and psychological satisfaction.
3. Sexual expression deepens existing love between a couple.
4. It is a much better means than masturbation to prepare an individual for a mature, loving and sharing sexual relationship.
5. It gives a couple the chance to develop sexual techniques that may be useful in marriage.
6. Sexual adjustment is easier when people are quite young than later on, in a marriage.
7. It prevents the development of homosexual tendencies, if that is desired.
8. If we think of it as totally natural, an individual goes against nature if he rejects it.
9. It permits a couple to determine in advance if they're likely to be sexually compatible in marriage.
10. It's wise to have a variety of sexual partners before marriage, because afterward such experimentation will be difficult, if not impossible, without divorce.

So much for the *pro* arguments. Here are the *cons,* the arguments against premarital intercourse:

1. There is danger of contracting VD.
2. There is always the possibility of pregnancy, no matter what kind of birth control is used.
3. Since such intercourse often takes place under dreary,

dangerous, or at least unromantic conditions, these surroundings can have a permanent effect on future attitudes toward sex, even after marriage.

4. When someone violates his personal code of ethics, he
   destroys his feeling of self-worth, and that can have a
   negative effect on his personality.

5. An otherwise good and promising relationship may
   break up if one member of the couple or both have
   feelings of guilt and loss of self-respect.

6. A girl who engages in premarital intercourse is twice as
   likely to engage in an adulterous relationship as the one
   who doesn't, Kinsey's research tells us.

7. If it is discovered, there may be rejection by parents,
   friends and others in the peer group.

8. Unfair as the double standard may be, there is always
   the risk that a man may lose his respect for the girl and
   reject her.

9. It is incorrect to assume, as many couples do, that a
   good sexual relationship guarantees adjustment to each
   other in other areas.

10. If there is no premarital intercourse, there is no basis to
    make an unfavorable comparison with marital inter-
    course.

At the University of Houston, where I teach a course called
Marriage, Family and Sex Education to as many as 1200 students
at one time, one of the questions I'm asked most frequently is,
"What would you tell your daughter (or son) about premarital
sex?" Of course I hear the same question from patients, and
I'm sure every psychologist who talks about sex problems hears
it constantly. A lot of people expect the professional to talk
out of both sides of his mouth, saying one thing publicly, but
another thing to his own children. It's a good question, and
here are my answers, beginning with the daughter:

I should say first that it's a question that can't be answered
completely in a short statement, because a whole lifetime of
living sets the stage for the answer. Nevertheless, we can make
an approach. I would begin with a healthy attitude toward sex
in the home; if the attitude is healthy at home it will be reflected in the children, and vice versa.

Granted that much, then, I would want my daughter to

know the biological and physiological facts about the sexual structure of male and female, to understand the similarities and differences between the sexes, much as I've explained them in this book. It's important that she should know the psychological makeup, too, understanding that males are more easily excited sexually than females, and by different methods and techniques. I'd want her to know what those techniques are, so she could avoid them in some situations and use them in others.

Parents have a major responsibility in maintaining consistency in sexual matters at home. A parent must feel at ease with his sexual ideas if he is to present the same attitude and approach to sex day in and day out. He should know and understand what his own attitudes are before he attempts to advise his children. It is very important for the mother and father to agree about these attitudes, so that they don't give their children different sets of ideas. Inconsistency only produces confusion and insecurity.

I would want my daughter to understand that there will be some inconsistencies between what she is taught at home and what society expects. She must realize that our society is filled with people who are against anyone who doesn't conform to their way of thinking and behaving, and that they will condemn and even persecute those who don't follow their rules.

I'd want her to know of methods and techniques of sexual outlet other than intercourse, and I would want her to know the values of those methods—for example, that masturbation and petting are perfectly normal ways of behavior that can and do satisfy sexual urges, and at the same time don't carry with them some of the problems that result from intercourse.

I would want her to have a kind and fair attitude toward other people, to be fair and ethical in all her relationships, including and especially sex. No cheating, no lying, no taking advantage of others. The place to draw the line in behavior, I would tell her, is when it harms another person or herself.

I would want her to understand that for many boys and young men sex is a game, and she ought to be prepared for lies and trickery. Seduction is an ego trip for boys and men who feel sexually inferior. At the same time, she should realize that this behavior is not something personal directed against her, but a reflection of society's disturbed attitude toward sex.

I would want her to understand the views of different religions, and to see how the unwise use of their ideas and ideals can produce harmful guilt and repression. I would make it clear how guilt creates devastating sexual conflicts, and urge her to avoid sex because of rational factors, and not because of guilt and repression.

If she decides on sexual intercourse, I would want her to know about and have access to contraceptive devices, and to have the best information on pregnancy and venereal diseases. (That kind of information, I think, should be made available to all children, at an early age.)

When it comes down to the hard question, I would tell her that basically I believe a girl (or a boy, for that matter) is better off if she avoids premarital intercourse, especially in the teens, and would be better advised to use masturbation or petting when sexual expression is necessary. But if, in spite of my beliefs, intercourse is her choice, I would want her to know that I was with her and that my respect and love would not change. I would hope that if she needed a friend, she would turn first to me or my wife, or both of us, and know that she could be sure of our support.

I have some reason to believe that these ideas work, because of my twenty-five years of teaching and counseling college students and because I raised my own daughter on these principles and she is now happily married. I haven't any idea whether she had premarital intercourse or not; I respect and love her too much even to question her on that point, although I know that if I did, she could answer without embarrassment to either of us. She has an open and healthy attitude toward sex, without the guilt or shame or fear which causes the repressions that build to peaks of intensity, erupting into sexual or neurotic acting out. Consequently I think she is likely to remain emotionally stable and healthy.

As to what I would tell my son, besides the same basic information that I would give a daughter, I would want him to have an understanding of the basic difference between the sexes in late adolescence, when young men between 17 and

21 are experiencing the height of their sex drive and consequently have a sound biological basis for their great interest in sex. Girls don't ordinarily have such a strong physical need and don't reach the peak of their drive until they're in *their* thirties. Therefore, when teenage girls become sexually involved with a boy it is usually because of emotional rather than sexual needs.

I would try to help him realize that an immature and maladjusted girl can easily persuade herself that a deep emotional relationship exists between her and a boy when sex is involved. She wants to believe they are in love, out of her desperate need for security. It would be his responsibility, I would point out, not to lead a girl purposefully into such a position, and to avoid entering that kind of relationship if he thought the girl was doing it for emotionally disturbed reasons.

I would want him to have the same advice as my daughter about premarital sex. If he should feel the need for sexual gratification, along with the other benefits of a close, warm relationship before marriage, he should consider the advantages of mutual masturbation and petting.

I would want my son to see the deep wrong involved in putting sex on a totally physical basis, and to think enough of himself so that he wouldn't want to share even a cup of coffee with a girl he didn't enjoy and like, much less to have so intimate an experience as sexual intercourse with her. I would hope that he would evaluate any girl in whom he was interested as a total person, according to what she was, what she did and believed in, rather than simply on the basis of whether or not she had ever had intercourse, or would or wouldn't have intercourse with him. By following that philosophy, he would have as much, if not more, respect for a girl after having any sexual experience with her as before. I would want my son to help the girl maintain her reputation in the community, which is so ready to frown on and criticize any girl who has sexual experiences, by keeping quiet about the sexual aspect of their relationship, by speaking favorably of her, and by continuing to treat her with respect and courtesy in public and in private.

Although I know it is not easy, I would advise him not to be unduly swayed by the immature bragging of other young men who, ignoring the rights and feelings of the girls involved, regard seduction as a measure of their masculinity and success as a person. Neither should he be influenced by their contempt or belittling if he refused to adopt similar neurotic patterns.

As for the question of premarital intercourse itself, he should have the same information and advice that I would give my daughter, with the added hope that by using his knowledge of techniques he would be able to give a girl as much pleasure and satisfaction as possible in whatever form of sexual relationship they might enter into. He should place her needs and satisfaction on an equal plane with his own, because when both partners take this approach, much greater fulfillment can be expected, not only in sex but in every other aspect of the relationship. I have given this advice to my son, who happens to be my close friend as a grown man, just as he was when he was a boy. I don't know what his sexual experiences have been either. I know his views on the matter, and he knows mine, and they are much the same. I think his attitudes are mature and healthy.

To sum it all up, I believe that neither partner is likely to be damaged by premarital intercourse—*if* they are believers in decency and fair play; *if* they have a mature, guilt-free attitude toward sex; *if* they have decided that they wish to go ahead only after a rational discussion, and not when they are caught up in the passion of sex play; and *if* they are mature enough to accept the responsibilities that go along with intercourse.

Unfortunately, not everybody has the kind of attitudes I've been talking about here, as is readily apparent when we get down to discussing marital heterosexual intercourse, which is the only kind of sexual activity, except erotic dreams, that is totally approved by our culture. Actually, while intercourse is the sexual outlet most frequently used by married couples, sexual relationships in about a half of all marriages are considered at least somewhat inadequate by those involved in them. One reason, clearly, is that too much is expected of sex in marriage. Young people who haven't had premarital experience hear so much about the glories and pitfalls of it, and much of what they hear is so wrong and distorted, that when they finally come to the marriage bed they have false hopes and expectation. That is why an adequate sex education is so important to sexual adjustment in marriage, because it puts the role of sex into proper perspective, making it neither more nor less important than it really is.

All but an extremely small number of married men participate at least occasionally in marital intercourse; this is true even of men in their late fifties. But that isn't the only way married men obtain their sexual release. A certain amount comes from such sources as masturbation and nocturnal emissions. Those with the lowest education get the highest portion of release through intercourse; those with the highest education are at the other end of the scale. The more highly educated men have the same amount of total sexual activity, but it is divided among several types of outlets such as petting, masturbation, and oral-genital sex as well as intercourse, while the less educated men are more likely to limit their sex to intercourse.

Frequency of sexual intercourse in marriage decreases with age, dropping from about four times a week when the husband is in his teens, to about three times a week when he reaches the age of 30, about two times a week at the age of 50, and about once a week at the age of 60. Of course, many men in their seventies and even eighties are capable of sexual intercourse. In spite of the decreasing frequency, among both men and women, those who have the strongest sex drive in their youth also have the greatest sexual capacity in old age.

Husbands with low education seldom have sexual foreplay before intercourse, but the average college-educated husband spends from 5 to 15 minutes, sometimes an hour or more, in petting before intercourse. College-educated men prefer to have intercourse in the nude and in a lighted room; the lower-educated groups prefer the opposite. Religiously active men appear to engage in marital intercourse less frequently than those who are less religiously devout.

Virtually all married women participate in sexual intercourse, as the men do, and again there is a gradual decline in frequency as the marriage progresses, probably as a result of the husband's decreasing sexual interest and capability, since the woman's sex drive remains fairly constant once its peak is reached in her early thirties.

The average frequency of marital intercourse is about three times a week among teenage females, about twice a week among women aged 30, about once a week among women 50 years of age, and about once every two weeks among women aged 60. (Remember, their husbands are usually older than they are.) The incidence of masturbation and nocturnal dreams involving orgasm increases after a woman marries, and remains fairly steady at its maximum level until she is 60 or older. During the first year of marriage, 75 percent of all women reach orgasm at least once during intercourse. The percentage gradually increases to 90 percent after 20 years of marriage.

Unlike the men, a woman's education has little bearing on the frequency of her marital intercourse, but in every age group, the higher the wife's education, the more likely she is to reach orgasm. Whether or not she is religiously devout seems to have little effect on the frequency of marital intercourse.

Some women, surprisingly, remain virgins after marriage, victims of ignorance or old wives' tales, or beset by a great number of emotional problems. They have a fear of pain associated with first sexual intercourse, or they believe that intercourse is nasty and wicked, or their husband is incapable of performing the act, or they fear pregnancy and childbirth, or they have an unusually small vagina. It may be hard to believe, but some are ignorant of the exact location of their sex organs.

As I've implied, not all marital sexual activity takes place between the partners, but the word "extramarital" doesn't necessarily mean adultery or even extramarital intercourse. As I have indicated, there are many sexual outlets other than intercourse which form the total picture of extramarital behavior. For purposes of discussion, however, let's limit ourselves right now to intercourse between a married person and someone other than the husband or wife.

Adultery is condemned in virtually every Western culture, both by religion and by law, because of the threat it poses to the family unit, but it is significant that at no time in the history of any culture has the male's extramarital intercourse been consistently controlled or severely punished, while women everywhere have been subjected to a much more rigid code of sexual ethics. Not only is this true, but at every social level wives are more permissive of their husbands' extramarital affairs than husbands are of their wives' adultery.

These facts simply reflect the belief that has prevailed since the dawn of history, which women are now challenging, that women have been regarded as more or less the property of their husbands. It has always been held as an article of faith that if women were to engage in extramarital intercourse, it would threaten the economic stability of society, reflect on the masculinity and social position of the husband, and in case of pregnancy, would raise the question of paternal responsibility —that is, the identity of the father, and who was to assume the father's responsibilities to the child.

In actual practice, the frequency of extramarital intercourse decreases with age among men, along with other kinds of sexual activity, but among women it increases. Since it is usually such a hidden activity, it is difficult to make anything more than an educated guess about the true incidence and frequency of adultery; it is often the last thing a person will admit, and even patients who have been in therapy for a long time and have a confidential relationship with a therapist often withhold the truth about extramarital intercourse.

Another result of the double standard is that the seriousness of the threat to a marriage because of adultery seems to be determined by whether it is the wife or the husband who is the offending party. A single adulterous act by the wife may very well do permanent damage to the marriage, while a similar act by the husband is often forgiven unless it is a lengthy affair in which he really loves the other woman. This difference is based on the notion that a married man can have sexual relation with a woman other than his wife for physical pleasure only, without necessarily any feelings of love, while it is assumed that a woman must be in love with the other man before she permits a sexual relationship with him.

People who enter adulterous affairs usually expect them to

provide the love, excitement, adventure, romance, vigor and return to youth that their marriages have not supplied. They are often profoundly disappointed, simply trading one set of problems for another. There is no question that adulterous affairs place an additional strain on any marriage, no matter what its status, and often cause more unhappiness than the experiences are worth.

Nevertheless, about three-fourths of all married men admit to at least an occasional desire to have such an affair, and at a conservative estimate, about half of them actually have such experiences at some point during their marriage. Men at the lowest educational level have more extramarital intercourse during the early years of marriage, and college men have less.

The most common cause of extramarital intercourse is the desire for sexual variety, and dissatisfaction with the sexual relationship they have at home. If a couple is willing to experiment, however, the desire for sexual variety can be satisfied within the marriage itself. Husband and wife should accept the idea that "anything goes" in their sexual relationship, as long as the activity adds to the pleasure of their sex life. Couples should introduce new and exciting techniques into their sex lives. If they can keep their sexual interest active and stimulated, neither is likely to be bored with the sex they have at home, or to seek sexual adventure outside the marriage.

About a quarter of the women who have reached the age of 40 have had extramarital intercourse, with the highest incidence among college-educated women. There is also a higher incidence among women who have had premarital intercourse (probably a reflection of their strong sex drives). The lowest incidence, obviously, is among the religiously devout.

Even as a teenager it's worth thinking about how to establish and maintain a good marriage relationship. In spite of some of the changing attitudes toward appropriate lifestyles for women, most girls look forward to marriage. But judging from the high incidence of divorce in America, particularly among teenagers and those in their early twenties, not many of them appear to know how to handle it when they achieve it. And of course the same thing can be said for the men.

It goes without saying, I think, that any relationship is successful only if the individuals involved bring to it such things as decency, maturity, unselfishness, fairness, and a genuine concern for others. The sexual relationship is special because it is the closest possible bond between two people, and carries with it hopes of fulfillment, both emotional and physical, that are possible in no other human relationship.

The sex drive itself is physiological, but human sexuality involves far more than the physical. To develop our sexuality to its highest level of personal gratification is something we have to work at. The most effective tools are a knowledge of what we're doing, an attitude toward sex that is free of guilt, a constant concern for the feelings of the partner and a determination that our own behavior will cause no harm to ourselves or to others. Add patience, courtesy, and a sense of humor, and you've filled the prescription.

Although it sounds obvious to say so, the beginning of a satisfying sexual relationship is to have a clean and attractive body. That doesn't mean handsome, or pretty. It means cleanliness of body and clothing, and taking the most advantage of whatever physical gifts we've been given. A man who is grossly overweight, doesn't shave often enough, dresses sloppily and stands in need of a mouthwash is not an irresistible sexual partner. A woman whose hair is lank and oily, or whose clothing is soiled, or who is guilty of urinal, vaginal or underarm odors paves the way for the loss of her husband's respect and admiration, and probably love as well. That doesn't mean such people can't and don't have sex; it means that they are likely to be able to have it only with people like themselves, and if one party to a marriage lets himself go this way, sexual difficulties are sure to follow.

While it's fashionable to sneer these days at marriage manuals as "how to" books, this kind of pseudosophistication is not founded on fact. As any therapist can testify, there are any number of people who enter marriage even in these supposedly enlightened days with little or no sexual experience, and even less knowledge of sexual techniques. It is popularly supposed that they, like anyone, can "learn on the job," so to speak. Wrong again; not many of them do. Instead they become victims of our society's sexual repressions and enforced ignorance.

Fortunately, authoritative information is now abundantly available—through books, lectures, and teachers—and those about to enter marriage would help themselves greatly by getting as much information as possible about sexual techniques. The fine points of a successful sexual relationship do *not* develop "instinctively," as is so often claimed. First attempts are likely to be more mechanical than spontaneous, but if they are armed with knowledge and can talk freely with each other about everything, early problems eventually dissolve and are replaced by comfort and satisfaction.

Intercourse fills the psychological and physiological needs of human beings in a way nothing else in marriage can do; consequently both husband and wife help their marriage immeasurably if they do everything in their power to make it as joyous and satisfactory as possible. Consider, for example, the variety of positions available in intercourse.

No one position of partners is more "normal" or more "acceptable" than others. That is the first lesson. It is hard to believe, but many people go through life thinking there is only one way that is right and proper—the so-called "missionary position," or Position One, with the man lying on top of the woman. In reality, this basic position is easily reversed. People can also have intercourse lying side by side facing each other, or with the woman, with her back to the man, on her side or her stomach, or sitting astride the man, or in a variety of other ways. Every couple ought to experiment to find the positions that give the greatest pleasure, and the one best suited for a particular occasion.

When you become older, especially at the time you are planning to be married, you will want to know a great deal more about how to arouse your partner sexually, how to get the most enjoyment out of the various sex acts, what the various sexual positions are, and how to use them. When you reach that time of your life, it will be the time when you and your future spouse will want to read and study the best marriage manual and "how-to-do-it" book available. There are many good books on the market but I would like to put in a plug for another of my own books, *Human Sexuality,** that will give you all the information along these lines you will ever need. Besides that, it contains detailed information on all aspects of human sexuality and there are over 700 references to books and scientific studies to support the material in the text.

Orgasm, or climax, is the summit of physical and emotional gratification in sexual activity. I suppose as much has been written about this part of the act as the act itself. It has been, and still is, a controversial subject in some respects. For years we've heard a great deal about the "tyranny of the orgasm," the idea being that our culture says you must have the orgasm, or else you're a failure. Entire books have been written on the subject of whether there is or is not such a thing as a vaginal orgasm, as opposed to a clitoral one, ever since Kinsey declared flatly in 1953 that the vaginal type did not exist. This conflict still rages, largely between the Freudian-oriented psychoanalysts and the newer breed, supported by the physiologists. Others who insist that there is only a clitoral orgasm have added considerably to this literature. Actually, an orgasm is both a mental and a physical reaction involving the brain and the entire body. It is foolish to speak of a vaginal or a clitoral orgasm since the entire body is involved, although it is true that most of the erotic nerve endings of a woman are in the clitoris and minor lips and those of a man are in the glans of the penis. No wonder the bewildered teenager so often asks, "Just what *is* an orgasm, anyway, and how do I know when I'm having one?" It's not a silly question; some boys and many girls *don't* know.

What it is can easily be defined. It is a highly pleasurable, tension-relieving, seizurelike response centered in the nerves, tissues and muscles of the genitals: that is, in the clitoris, vagina and uterus in the woman; and the prostate, seminal vesicles and penis in the man. This physical and psychological arousal, leading to the convulsive release we call orgasm, also involves a good many other reactions in the body besides those in the

---

* *Human Sexuality* is available from the same publishers of this book, Van Nostrand Reinhold, 430 West 33rd Street, New York, N.Y. 10001.

pelvic area. There is a marked rise in blood pressure and heart rate; the breath comes faster and deeper; there is engorgement of special tissues with blood; and finally, there is an explosive release of muscular and nervous tension.

Whatever the variation may be in individuals, and it is a wide one, orgasm is usually a brief experience lasting only 3 to 10 seconds, although it may seem longer. People who find it difficult to understand the intensity of orgasm should imagine what it would be like if any other urgent need of the body were to be satisfied in an equally short time. For instance, can you imagine the sensation of satisfying an overwhelming hunger for food in a period of 5 or 10 seconds, rather than the 20 or 30 minutes usually occupied in eating a meal?

There are many more similarities than differences in the orgasmic response of men and women, and the pleasure each derives from it. The most significant differences are that male orgasm is accompanied by ejaculation, and that women are capable of several orgasms during a sexual experience, while men usually are not. There is also a wide variation among women in the strength and duration of their orgasmic experience, while there is more consistency among men.

Most men almost always achieve orgasm through sexual intercourse. On the other hand, many women can't have orgasm through intercourse, but they can through other methods of stimulation such as masturbation.

A man usually achieves orgasm within about 4 minutes after intercourse begins, while a woman may need from 10 to 20 minutes of intercourse before she attains orgasmic response —if she is able to achieve it at all in this manner. But with various methods of direct stimulation of the clitoris and vulva (again, manual stimulation, for example), usually less than 4 minutes is needed to bring a woman to orgasm.

In their landmark study of human sexual response, the research team of Masters and Johnson have described with scientific precision, for the first time, the physiological reactions that both men and women experience during the various phases of sexual stimulation, leading to climax. They divide these reactions into four phases:

1. The *excitement phase,* the beginning of sexual arousal, varies in length from a few minutes to hours, depending on the type and intensity of the sexual stimulus, and on the degree of freedom from negative stimuli, such as noise, fear of discovery, hostility toward the partner, and other possible obstacles like these. During this phase, the woman's breasts may increase in size greatly, and the nipples of both males and females usually become erect and stand out. Many women and some men develop a measleslike rash over the neck, throat, chest and stomach. A noticeable increase in both voluntary and involuntary muscle tension and in blood pressure and heart rate begins during this phase. The clitoris and the penis become enlarged and erect.

During this phase, the first indication of a woman's sexual excitement, vaginal "sweating," occurs. This sweating phenomenon takes place within 10 to 30 seconds after excitement begins, and serves to lubricate the vagina to permit easy penile penetration. That's why girls notice their panties are wet after a necking session, even though they don't go beyond kissing. The major and minor vaginal lips become enlarged and thicken because of engorgement of blood. In the man, the skin of the scrotum thickens and the testicles are pulled closer to the body.

2. The *plateau phase,* the high level of sexual excitement experienced just before orgasm occurs, is reached through a continuation of the stimulation that was effective in bringing about and maintaining the first phase. Muscular tension, blood pressure and heart rate continue to increase in both men and women. The cords of the neck may stand out, and there will probably be a straining of face, hands and feet. The outer third of the vagina becomes congested with blood, its ring of muscles contracts, and the opening of the vagina may be reduced significantly. Excitement during this phase causes the uterus to pull up into the abdominal cavity, producing a ballooning or tenting effect that enlarges the inner portion of the vagina. Blood continues to swell the region of the vulva, and the testicles become engorged with blood and increase in size from 50 to 100 percent. Cowper's glands in the man, and Bartholin's glands in the woman, secrete two or three drops of

fluid during this phase. At the end of this phase, the body and glans of the clitoris withdraw from their overhang position and pull back deeply beneath the hood that covers the clitoral body, and the rate of respiration increases sharply.

3. The *orgasmic phase*, orgasm itself, is reached when the arousal techniques of the first two phases are continued. It lasts, as I've said, for an extremely short time, generally from 3 to 10 seconds, although sometimes longer in women. Men vary little in their orgasmic response but women vary enormously, individually and as a group in the strength and duration of orgasm. For some it is a mild experience. For others it is so intense that they become unaware of their surroundings. During this phase, muscular tension, heart rate and blood pressure reach their greatest height in both sexes.

In the male, contractions of the prostate, vas deferens, and seminal vesicles trigger ejaculation, meaning the forcible ejection of the seminal fluid through and out of the urethra. In both men and women there are short contractions at intervals of about eight-tenths of a second in the genital and anal regions, although the intervals between contractions lengthen after the first few.

One thing everybody can agree on about the sex act is that its most highly pleasurable sensations are experienced during this phase, whether they are relatively mild or emerge in a wild paroxysm of passion.

4. The *resolution phase* marks the return of the sexual system to its normal, nonstimulated state. The length of this phase is directly proportionate to the length of the excitement phase; the longer the latter lasts, the longer the resolution lasts. All the changes that occurred during the first two phases now disappear, in the reverse order in which they developed. About a third of both men and women develop a widespread film of perspiration, which is especially apparent on the forehead, around the mouth, under the arms, and sometimes over the chest, back and thighs. This reaction is apparently not related to physical exertion, since it occurs regardless of the degree of exertion during the first three phases.

There is one important difference between men and women in their response during this phase. After orgasm, the man enters a *refractory period,* as it is called, a temporary state during which he resists further sexual stimulation. Techniques that were effective and pleasurable just a little time before are now ineffectual, and even distasteful. Women, however, do not usually have such a period.

This is a difference that sometimes causes trouble in sex relations, if neither partner understands what is happening. An old French saying puts it in a more literary way, freely translated: "After loving, all animals are sad." But the man is sadder for a while, with all passion spent. If men only knew it, a woman would be satisfied to be held tenderly at this point, and talked to in the same fashion. Nothing kills the good effects of the sex act more than the man who turns over and quickly goes to sleep or who immediately jumps out of bed and goes about his business, leaving his partner alone, possibly even unsatisfied. The same is true, of course, of the woman who is in too much of a hurry to douche or bathe. The good lover cuddles, and talks, and perhaps even has some more sex, not necessarily full intercourse, in a little while. This occurs naturally, of course, when two people really love each other and have built up a warm, intimate relationship.

I should say something, too, about the subject of simultaneous orgasm, since earlier sex manuals preached the idea that the greatest possible sexual pleasure could be gained only this way, and no doubt many thousands of couples have struggled to attain this blissful state, often without success. It is, unfortunately, an uneven business, for good physiological reasons.

At the onset of orgasm, the man's tendency is to plunge into the vagina as deeply as possible and to hold this position for a few moments, to be followed perhaps by one or two deep deliberate thrusts. But the woman's desire is to continue, perhaps at an accelerated rate, the stroking plunging movements of the arousal phases. Since both patterns of movement cannot be carried out simultaneously, the sexual pleasure of one partner is obviously going to suffer. Since the most rewarding part of sexual intercourse is very likely to be the giving by one partner to the other of the fullest measure of concern and satisfaction, there would seem to be a better argument *against* rather than *for* simultaneous orgasms. Not that there's anything wrong with the simultaneous response. It has its own obvious merits, and if the idea appeals to a couple who have learned to control their responses, there is no reason why they can't try to do it as often as they like.

In spite of their greater capacity for orgasm, it is unfortunately true that women don't reach orgasm as easily as men do. "Unfortunately," I might add, only when men don't understand this and make the necessary adjustments.

Psychological blocks seem to make the difference, in most cases. That's understandable when we consider the taboos society imposes on a girl for the first twenty or so years of her life. Girls grow up in a world in which public sexual attitudes are at least outdated, if not directly in contradiction to the facts. The double standard is probably the worst example, along with the "shame" and "sin" that moralists attach to any aspect of human sexuality. It is easy for such attitudes to become the pathway to sexual conflicts in both partners, but especially in women. Another powerful inhibitor, of course, is the woman's fear of becoming pregnant.

At least things are better now. It has been only during the past half-century or so that the gratification of women has become a goal to be worked toward in sexual relationships. But even today some girls are still brought up with the idea that to enjoy their sexuality is immodest, animalistic, or unwomanly. No wonder these girls have difficulty responding sexually on any level.

Men, however, are not so restricted by the psychological barriers that hinder women. The double standard favors them, and so they are able to derive pleasure from sexual activity more easily than women. Only when our society arrives at a sexual ethic based on reason rather than shame—an ethic equally applicable to both sexes—will men and women be able to enjoy sexuality equally.

I hope no one will conclude from this discussion of orgasm that it must accompany every sexual experience if a couple is to have sexual compatibility or a happy marriage. That simply isn't so, for either partner. No one can deny the great physical and emotional pleasure of orgasm, but it is by no means crucial to a happy and fulfilled life. Overrating its importance can lead to conflicts that are damaging to the enjoyment of intercourse, and to the emotional relationship between husband and wife.

If most other aspects of a marriage are satisfactory, if there are shared interests, naturalness, mutual respect, the desire to please, and open lines of verbal communication—a wife may be happy even though she is sexually unresponsive to some degree.

Not every man understands this simple fact. Some think their wives must respond to them with the same frequency and intensity they exhibit. They may be led to believe this because of premarital or extramarital involvement with women whose sexual desire and response are powerful. They should remember that the very strength of the sexual drive in some women may propel them into nonmarital sexual acts, while their wives simply may not have such strong sexual needs. Such a wife may be no less loving of her husband, or any the less concerned about the marriage.

This chapter has dealt almost entirely with the physiologic aspects of human sexuality. That doesn't mean the emotional aspects are less important. A close human relationship and deep emotional involvement are of the very first importance to a complete and fulfilling sexual experience. If someone asks you, "What is love?" or "How do you know you're in love?", that kind of relationship and involvement are the best ways I know of answering those questions.

Remember that the physiological sex drive can be relieved without love, closeness, or even understanding, but no one can really attain complete emotional, physical and sexual satisfaction without those primary elements.

10

Difference in sexual behavior

SOMEONE ONCE ASKED DR. KINSEY to define a nymphomaniac. "Why, yes," he answered amiably, "a nymphomaniac is someone who has more sex than you do." In his wry way, Kinsey was saying that too many people are ready to classify any sexual activity different from their own as abnormal or perverted. Anthropology shows us that what is usual in one culture may be quite unusual in another. Consequently, certain sexual acts may be different from "ordinary" sexual behavior and may be branded as abnormal, but such unusual behavior should never be considered a perversion simply because it is out of the ordinary in a particular culture. The more scientists dis-

149

cover about sexual behavior, in fact, the less they're inclined to label any unusual expression as "abnormal."

For instance, it is generally accepted by sexologists that about 70 percent of American males will engage in some kind of sexual act during their lifetimes that will be illegal under some law, somewhere in the country. (Kinsey often observed that if existing sex laws were strictly enforced, most of the people in the nation would be liable to prosecution if they were caught.) About 60 percent of these males will engage in such behavior on a fairly frequent basis during some period of their lives.

We don't expect everybody to like asparagus, and we don't expect those who do like it to want it all the time. The same kind of flexible attitude toward such individual tastes should also apply to human sexual behavior. No one has the moral right, and he should not have the legal right, to force his sexual preferences on others. Even if we personally find some sexual expressions unacceptable, we shouldn't consider them abnormal or perverted as long as what is done is not harmful to the partners, is carried out by consenting adults without force or threat, and takes place out of sight and sound of unwilling observers.

It has become increasingly difficult for scientists to define abnormal sexual behavior, although the moralists and legislators don't seem to have any trouble. "Sexual perversion" is a phrase often used more for convenience than for any exact definition, with some exceptions, of course. Under the heading of "abnormalities" (I am going to call them sexual variances, which is much more accurate), we usually include sexual behavior that is illegal (like rape), or is not illegal but is generally regarded as immoral, even if both partners are willing (like sadistic or cruel acts), or that is, in a broader sense, sexual failure that constitutes individual misfortune (like the inability of a man to perform the sex act, or of a woman to enjoy it).

In trying to sort out such a complicated and ambiguous subject, I am going to divide sexual variances into three types: Those acts that are considered unusual or "abnormal" in themselves, those in which the sexual partner is not an accepted or usual choice, and those in which the sex drive or desire itself is either unusually strong or weak. Let's begin with the sex acts that are themselves considered "abnormal," remembering that there are differing viewpoints about "abnormality," in which the law and public attitudes may be on one side in some cases, and the opinions of some scientists on the other. Also remember that many of the causes of mental or emotional problems are in the unconscious mind and the person involved is not aware of why he does what he does.

Sadism is a case in point. The law and most people agree that the sexual pleasure a person gains by inflicting either physical or psychological pain upon his partner in a sexual relationship is abnormal. It is named after the Marquis de Sade (1740–1814), whose books about his sexual adventures centered on the whipping and other kinds of torture that gave him sexual pleasure. Recently De Sade and more modern writers on the subject have had a new popularity in books and motion pictures, and on the stage, where the Theatre of Cruelty is a subject of intellectual interest and debate. But while a movie showing a man whipping or otherwise abusing a woman is termed pornographic in a setting where sexual gratification is plainly the object, the same scene with the sexual references removed in one of the more violent legitimate Hollywood productions is considered entertainment.

Sadism may involve inflicting physical pain through whipping, biting or slapping, or psychological pain through hurtful or cruel remarks. The latter kind is so common that if it were interpreted literally, a large part of the population could be classified as sadists. Sadists, from a clinical point of view, have often been taught as children, either consciously or unconsciously, to have disgust for anything sexual; their later acts of cruelty are meant to punish their partners for engaging in anything so shameful. Sometimes the sadist attempts to cope with feelings of inferiority, his sadistic acts reassuring him that he is more powerful than his partner.

Masochism is the mirror image of sadism, in which a person gets sexual pleasure from being hurt, physically or mentally, by his sexual partner. This behavior also got its name from a writer, the Austrian novelist Leopold von Sacher-Masoch (1836–1895), who had a long history of masochistic involvements with women.

Like sadism, masochism develops from an attitude of shame and disgust toward normal heterosexual relationships. The masochist often uses the pain inflicted on him to counteract the guilt he feels because of his sexual desires. In other cases, he believes that his ability to endure punishment demonstrates his strength and superiority, or otherwise makes him the center of attention. At still other times, he may be so fearful of rejection that he allows himself to be subjected to almost any humiliation or punishment that will please his partner and win for him, as he sees it, affection and acceptance. According to some interpretations, the masochist considers suffering necessary to pleasure, since in his past experiences pain and sexual pleasure are somehow connected.

Sadism and masochism are found more frequently among men than women, in spite of the fact that women are popularly thought of as being more masochistic. Then too, once more, the line between normality and abnormality is rather fine. Some people are aggressive in their lovemaking, and biting and hurting become part of it, although we still consider this normal. The clinical definition is that it becomes abnormal when a person actually seeks to inflict physical pain or verbal abuse on another to increase sexual pleasure, or wishes to have the pain or abuse inflicted on himself for the same reason.

As one might expect, sadists and masochists often find each other as sexual partners. It was one of Kinsey's more interesting discoveries that in these situations, it is the masochist and not the sadist who controls and regulates the sexual activity.

Exhibitionism, which causes 35 percent of all arrests for sexual violations, is clearly defined as a sexual problem. It meets the definition fully because exhibitionists get sexual gratification from exhibiting their genitals to an *unwilling* observer. Far more men than women are in this category, at least in a legal sense; we rarely hear of a woman being arrested for exhibitionism. The public is much more tolerant of the exposed bodies of women than of men. One can imagine the outcry if men had adopted styles as revealing as the mini- and micro-skirt, or the later ones exposing the breasts.

Exhibitionists are usually filled with feelings of insignificance or inadequacy, and hope to gain the attention they crave through exhibiting themselves. Typically, an exhibitionist is a quiet, timid, submissive man whom people are likely to describe as "nice" but immature. He is often the product of a family upbringing that was overstrict and puritanical in its attitudes toward sex, and particularly he has suffered from the domination of a powerful, overprotective mother. Most exhibitionists are married, but their sexual relationship with their wives is likely to be poor. All these influences combine to create a marked fear about their masculinity.

Obviously, the exhibitionist hopes his actions will greatly shock his viewer, and his gratification is complete if that is the reaction of the viewer; nothing disappoints or discourages him so much as indifference. A girl confronted by an exhibitionist acts sensibly if she calmly ignores him. The reader should be reminded that to want one's sexual partner to see and enjoy one's nude body and genitals (and vice versa) is a perfectly normal thing. It becomes a sexual problem when the person exhibits his genitals to an *unwilling* observer.

In *voyeurism,* we are back again on ambiguous ground, since there is something of the voyeur in nearly everybody, in varying degrees, and it is hard to separate this natural component from what is clinical. Voyeurism is defined as behavior in which erotic pleasure is gained by observing sexual acts or by looking at genitals or nudes. Since a great many people show that behavior, we have to say it becomes a sexual problem only when it is the *only* means of sexual gratification, or is the preferred means.

"Peeping Tom" is the popular name that has long been given to the voyeur, and that describes his activity, peering secretly under drawn windowblinds, boring peepholes in walls and doors of bedrooms or toilets, or spying on the sexual activities of others. Voyeurs are rarely women because, as we have seen earlier, most women are not greatly stimulated visually. In its clinical sense, voyeurism is believed to develop as the individual's defense against what he thinks is a threat to his sexual adequacy. By only observing sexual objects and activities, he guards against any personal failure in intercourse, or he avoids what he has been taught is "bad" or "dirty."

Transvestism is sexual pleasure gained from dressing in the clothes of the opposite sex. People usually think that transvestites are homosexual, or have such tendencies, but this behavior is found just as frequently in heterosexuals, asexuals (those attracted to neither sex), and bisexuals (those attracted to both sexes). Actually, the transvestite likes being the sex he is; he simply likes to wear the clothes of the opposite sex. In the sexual act he, like any heterosexual person, wants a partner of the opposite sex.

This kind of activity usually begins in early childhood, and is often caused by parental rejection of the child's sex.

There is some ambiguity to be found here, too, because extremely unattractive women, for example, may attempt to make their condition less obvious by dressing in men's clothing, but on the other hand, women can and do wear masculine clothing these days without any social disapproval. Real transvestism is rare in women, however, and the public's chief objection to male transvestites is apparently based on the erroneous assumption that they are homosexual. This, in turn, rises from the equally incorrect popular belief that all male homosexuals are effeminate, although only about 15 percent of them are, and that homosexuality is immoral and bad; consequently any display of effeminacy is bad and immoral.

Transvestites who want to lead more usual lives can sometimes learn to do so through psychotherapy, but a much greater problem exists for those men and women who want to belong to the opposite sex. We call them *transsexual*. They are often confused with transvestites, but the distinction between them is an easy one to remember. Transvestites, almost always men, like their sex organs but like to cross-dress in women's clothing because they feel sensual in them, and because they are sexually excited by feminine clothing. The transsexual, on the other hand, is usually a male, although a few are female, but he does not like his sex organs and wants those of the opposite sex. He feels that nature played a dirty trick on him by putting him into a body of the wrong sex. Sometimes he actually does change sex through surgery and with the help of hormone therapy. Transsexuals who are not able to obtain surgery may wear the clothes of the other sex and even try to pass as members of the opposite sex, sometimes without being detected.

We come now to the category of variation from the normal in which the choice of sexual partner, either a person or an object, is a departure from the norm.

Foremost on this list is *homosexuality,* which means sexual attraction to a member of the same sex, usually resulting in sexual relations. Male homosexuals outnumber female homosexuals (or lesbians) about two or three to one, although the reason for this is a matter of debate and some researchers have challenged the figure.

As I've noted, the popular belief that all male homosexuals are effeminate and all females masculine, or "butch," has no basis in fact. There are no physical characteristics common to all homosexuals, but too often frail or passive men and aggressive or robust women are unfairly branded as homosexuals when they are not. It is not at all unusual to find very masculine appearing men and very feminine women who are leading active homosexual lives. Only 15 percent of homosexual males are easily identified by their appearance, as I remarked earlier, and even fewer lesbians can be so identified (only about 5 percent).

Theories about why people become homosexual are abundant, and not one of them has been proved. Highly qualified therapists, scientists and researchers differ, sometimes quite violently, on this subject. There are schools that believe it is the result of hereditary tendencies, environmental influences, or sex hormone imbalances. Some argue that it must be inborn, since most homosexuals grow up in a culture that encourages heterosexuality, and are usually ignorant of their tendencies until they are adolescent and encounter opportunities for homosexual attachments. This, it is said, proves that they were born with such tendencies and did not acquire them.

Another, and perhaps more convincing, argument is that homosexuality is an outgrowth of environmental circumstances. An individual may seek homosexual outlets, for instance, as a result of an accidental but pleasurable homosexual incident in childhood, or because of having been segregated with others of the same sex for long periods of time, such as in a boarding school or correctional institution. Unsatisfactory social relationships with members of the opposite sex may also cause a person to seek the companionship of his own sex, and thus avoid the possibility of similar failures in the future.

If this argument is correct, we would certainly have to call the attitudes of parents the most powerful environmental pressure. Faulty attitudes toward sex, obvious marital unhappiness, or rejection of the child's sex by his parents may set the stage for homosexuality in a child. Furthermore, if the child has fears of incest because of confusing the mother with all women or the father with all men, hostility toward the parent of the opposite sex, or strong attraction toward the parent of the same sex, any of these factors, or a combination of them may create an atmosphere so threatening that the individual attempts eventually to escape through homosexuality.

Therapists who study the family lives of homosexuals often find disturbed patterns in them. Typically, the mother is unhappy in her marriage and turns to her son and develops a close and intimate relationship with him. Because of his wife's preference for the son, the father comes to resent him and discourages his masculine growth, while at the same time he shows a favoritism toward his daughter, if he has one.

Physiologists largely reject the above theories and believe that homosexuality is the result of an imbalance of sex hormones. The urine of a normal man or woman carries the hormones of both sexes, but one dominates the other. If the dominance is reversed, these researchers suggest, homosexuality results. This theory is plausible enough but it has little scientific investigation to support it.

Finally, it has been theorized by one of the three leading

authorities on the subject that homosexuality results from what he terms "ego modeling," a complex concentration of various forces on the growing child which push him in one direction or the other. This, too, awaits further investigation.

What we do know for sure about homosexuals is that they have no more serious personality problems than one would expect to find in the normal population. They can be as religious, moralistic, loyal to country or cause, rebellious and revolutionary, inhibited, bigoted, and critical of other kinds of sexual variation as anyone else. They are likely to be more concerned with their anxiety and fear of discovery than they are about their homosexual behavior.

Probably a majority of therapists now believe that people who are exclusively homosexual and who have never had or desired to have heterosexual contact cannot be changed by any medical or psychological means, and few want to be. Some therapists, mostly Freudians, dispute this vehemently. But it customarily turns out that homosexuals who are turned away from their behavior were really pseudo-homosexuals— that is, people who have turned to members of their own sex for love, affection, and sexual expression bcause they fear members of the opposite sex, even when they prefer them.

Our culture severely condemns male homosexuality, although it is gradually beginning to shift somewhat from this rigid attitude. As for female homosexuality, it is usually ignored. Men who react violently to homosexuality, with fists or words, are likely to have an underlying fear of their own homosexual tendencies; those who don't feel threatened by any such underlying tendencies are more understanding.

Society in general overreacts to the homosexual seduction of a child between the ages of 7 and 16. The effects, in fact, are seldom permanent, and these boys are no more likely to become homosexuals than boys who have not been seduced. The evidence is that they marry and lead quite normal lives.

This is true in almost all cases in which a child—male or female—is seduced by an adult. A preference for children as sexual partners is known as *pedophilia*. In pedophilia, adults get erotic pleasure from sexual relationships of one kind or another with children. Of all sex offenders, about a third are classed as pedophiles, and almost all of them are men. Only about 20 percent use physical violence, yet public reaction is stronger against a pedophile than against a rapist. Oddly enough, the pedophile himself usually has strict Victorian attitudes toward sex, believing firmly in the double standard, judging women as being either "good" or "bad," and insisting that their brides, but not themselves, be virgins. The pedophile is characteristically mentally dull, psychotic, and alcoholic with a general insensitivity to other people.

It is curious and distressing to observe that imprisoned sex offenders, in general, express strong religious convictions. They consider themselves very devout, respect the ministry, and read the Bible regularly. Indeed, almost all sex offenders admit to having received religious training in childhood, but very few report that they ever got any sex education from their parents. Obviously, then, religious training alone did not constitute a sufficient control over their unacceptable sexual behavior, but sex education from the proper source might have done so.

A person may seek sexual contact with a child because of his failure in normal personal and heterosexual relationships, especially with a sexually experienced adult. The child doesn't threaten his sexual abilities or frighten him psychologically, while adults do. He can, however, be reached and often treated effectively through psychotherapy.

In the opinion of most psychologists, sexual experiences at the hands of a pedophile are less disturbing to the child than to his parents. If parents can bring themselves to deal with such an event in a calm manner, the child usually suffers no lasting upset.

Another and quite different kind of sexual variance is *bestiality*, meaning sexual gratification obtained by engaging in sexual relationships with animals. It is far more common, naturally, among men brought up on farms, and such behavior in rural societies where there are few women probably has no more significance than masturbation as a sexual release. It is rare for women to have sexual experiences with animals, although it is far from unknown.

Most bestiality is a casual experience, but if it becomes a regular method of sexual release, it may mean the individual is trying to avoid possible failure in relationships with the opposite sex. In many cases, the individual shows his hostility or contempt toward women by identifying them with animals, or by choosing animals in preference to them.

Viewing *pornography* is hardly an abnormality, in any true meaning of the word, but the law considers it so. From a clinical standpoint, the viewing of written material or pictures deliberately designed to cause sexual excitement, which is the definition of pornography, can only be considered abnormal when it is the single or preferred method of sexual release.

For years we have had an increasing struggle, which shows no signs of diminishing, on the question of whether pornography is harmful to the young. No one denies that it can stimulate an individual sexually, no matter what his age, but there is no research evidence or clinical studies to support the belief that pornography causes sexual abnormalities or violence, nor is there any likelihood that it will cause excessive or abnormal sexual behavior. When such evidence appears, it turns out that tendencies toward that kind of behavior were already present in the individual before he ever came into contact with any pornographic material.

A strong response to pornography is directly related to youthfulness, and to a vivid imagination and sensitivity, which increase with education. Sex offenders respond *less* to pornography than nonoffenders, probably because they are not well educated and not young. Other objections to pornographic material include the charge that most of it shows a lack of good taste and literary value, but if the same standards were applied to a good many other kinds of creative activity, the same charge could be made.

Interest in pornography might conceivably diminish if sex education removed a sufficient quantity of anxiety and curiosity from people's minds, but considering the fact that as an art form, whatever its quality, it has existed for thousands of years, even this proposition seems dubious. It is also true that some of the world's greatest artists have painted pictures which are pornographic by any standard and are never shown in museums, yet are artistically superb. The same thing can be said for literature. Perhaps the best thing that could happen to pornography would be popular and legal recognition of its right to exist, in the hope that it would be generally raised to the level of the art it can demonstrably be.

Denmark provides an example of the lack of effect of pornography on a culture. In 1969, all the laws against pornography were removed, and sex crimes fell immediately by 31 percent. Pornography was available in good movie theaters on the most fashionable street, it was freely in evidence in bookstores, and it could be viewed in live exhibitions. The morality of the country did not fall apart; in fact, Denmark is a far more moral country than America. Although audiences and buyers were predominantly tourists, the movie audiences also contained many Danes, who ate their popcorn and were amused by the more pretentious scenes. This healthy situation was diminished in 1973 by a conservative Parliament's fear of "bad publicity."

Obscenity, like pornography, is a legal definition, or an attempt at it, and is not a description of a clinical condition or situation. In legal terms, it means words, gestures, pictures or actions that are considered offensive according to "community standards," as the law puts it, meaning general ideas of morality. Sometimes these are genuine nuisances, like the obscene phone call in which the caller uses explicit sexual terms designed to frighten and shock an unknown woman. Like the exhibitionist, the person who makes obscene phone calls is afraid of real contact with a woman. He is usually a pathetic, harmless man who can only get sexual pleasure from his calls. The calls are often accompanied by fantasies and masturbation. Expressions of shock only satisfy this kind of caller, and the best thing to do is to hang up and report the call to the telephone company. While the calls are annoying, girls should remember that they don't have to listen. Hanging up promptly will usually discourage a caller after a few times.

Crude writing and pictures on walls in public places annoy some people too, and invade their privacy, in a sense, but this mode of obscenity is much harder to combat, and in any case is a practice that goes back to ancient times.

Both pornography and obscene conduct are illegal in all states, in varying degrees, with interpretations and penalties varying widely, as we'll see in the final chapter. Both are usually in the eye, or mind, of the beholder. What is art to one person is pornography to another, and what is an honest expressive phrase to one is obscenity to another. If they damage an individual, it is because they fall on previously prepared and receptive soil, since they cannot of themselves produce damage.

Fetishism is a sexual variance in which the sex drive is directed toward a symbolic substitute for a human. The symbol can be an article, like underclothing or shoes, or a part of the body, like hair or feet. Fetishists, who are almost always male, may go so far as to commit burglary or even assault in the process of obtaining their sex symbols. These objects are associated with sexual excitement, or with the love and acceptance the fetishist once got from his mother or another female who was important in his life.

Ordinarily, fetishism is harmless enough, but there are two varieties of it which are not, *kleptomania* and *pyromania*, because they involve other people. Kleptomania is compulsive (that is, uncontrollable) stealing, usually of an article which has no value to the thief except as a sex symbol. Not all kleptomaniacs are fetishists, since this condition can have some complicated psychic causes. Typically, they are emotionally disturbed women who are filled with feelings of being unloved and unwanted. Sometimes they are boys or young men who steal women's undergarments, particularly panties.

Pyromania is far more dangerous. It is compulsive firesetting, that often has sexual roots. The relationship between sex and fire is expressed in our common phrases, "in heat" or "getting hot." Sexual excitement occurs when the pyromaniac, always a man and usually young, sets the fire, or watches the early stages of the blaze. He usually feels guilty afterwards and frequently makes attempts to put out the fire. A large number of these fetishists are emotionally disturbed.

Frottage is a clinical word I'm sure is unfamiliar to you, but if you live in a large city, you will probably know what it is when I explain that it is the act of rubbing or pressing against a person, usually a stranger, for the purpose of obtaining sexual pleasure. Such a person is called a frotteur, and he carries on his activity in crowded public places—elevators, subway cars, buses, wherever people are pressed together in crowds. The frotteur is something like the exhibitionist. He is, at his worst, an unappealing, inadequate man who would probably be frightened by the opportunity for a sexual relationship with an adequate adult woman.

Incest is sexual intercourse between two persons who are too closely related by blood or affinity, meaning kinship through marriage, to be legally married. Like so many other sex laws, those concerning incest vary tremendously from state to state and are often highly confusing, so that first cousins, for example, may marry in one state and not in another.

Incest may not appear in the courts very often (only 6 percent of all those arrested for sex offenses are charged with it), but it occurs far more frequently, in various ways, than the average citizen realizes. It is more likely to occur in families of low socio-economic levels than in others. Those who commit incest against children usually come from a slumlike home background, show a preoccupation with sex, drink heavily, and are often unemployed, giving them considerable time at home with the children.

Those who commit incest against adults are typically conservative, moralistic, restrained, religiously devout, traditional and uneducated. The most common form in this category is probably sexual relations between brother and sister, particularly in low-income families where children of both sexes have to share a bedroom. Next most common is father-daughter incest. Mother-son incest is rare in our contemporary society, although it was not uncommon in ancient times. There is reason to believe that it may be higher than we suspect even now, because when it takes place, it is not likely to be reported by either party.

The third pattern of sexual variations concerns those whose sexual desire is abnormally strong or weak.

To begin at the extreme of weakness, there is *frigidity,* a condition in which a woman has a total or partial lack of sex drive. Men are rarely frigid. In women, "frigidity" is usually considered a sign of sexual disorder.

Frigidity can be caused by physical or psychological factors. In the first category are such difficulties as disease, injuries, inborn defects in the genitals, and excessive use of drugs or alcohol. Common psychological causes include husbands who are "marital morons," as the phrase goes, because of their selfishness, overeagerness, or stupidity, all of which strangle romance and fill wives with repulsion toward sex; or resentment or anger on the part of wives toward their husbands. Any number of factors can interfere with the total relationship between husband and wife, and can cause problems in their sexual relationship as well. Frigidity is a poor choice of terms for this problem because many women labeled frigid may enjoy sex tremendously through the excitement and plateau phases of the sexual response cycle only to be unable to reach the orgasmic phase. Furthermore, many women are called frigid simply because their interest in sex is less than that of their husbands, even though they are capable of orgasms.

The most common and by far the most important sources of so-called frigidity are our old psychological enemies—shame, guilt and fear. Many women in our culture are taught from an early age, either directly or by implication, to consider sexual relations, whether in marriage or not, as evil and something to be avoided. A woman may also be fearful of becoming pregnant, or she may have homosexual tendencies, or she may have hostility toward men in general, or fear rejection or condemnation by her husband if she lets herself go sexually. All these things can prevent her from responding warmly to her husband.

Fortunately, this problem can be eliminated if it is handled with patience by both husband and wife through self-therapy, in addition to any medical or psychological treatment that seems advisable.

Another kind of problem is *impotency,* which means a man's inability to perform the sexual act, regardless of his desire. It involves his inability to attain or maintain an erection.

The underlying reasons are much the same as those that cause frigidity in a woman—some defect in the reproductive or central nervous system (very rare), fear, shame, or conscious or unconscious disgust, anger or hostility toward the wife. Most often the reason is psychological; there are few cases of physiological impotence.

Emotional upset of one kind or another sets the stage for impotency, and fear is its most common underlying cause—fear that sexual activity will be discovered, or that the woman will get pregnant, or that the man will acquire VD, or (most often) that he will fail in the attempt at intercourse. Next most common are feelings of guilt and shame, usually related to some childhood experience, or the result of faulty sex education. Feelings of inferiority and inadequacy will also interfere with a man's ability to get an erection, especially if he has had one or two failures before, as happens to every man from time to time. Many older men believe, mistakenly, that they have grown too old to function sexually, and they convince themselves to the point of becoming actually impotent. In reality, there is no physiological reason, barring ill health, why men cannot have an erection as long as they live.

When the causes are physical, impotence can be treated in several ways—by pills, injections, hormones, rest or surgery. If it is psychological impotence, however, which is far more likely, a more delicate approach is required, in which the wife assumes a role of great importance. If understanding and co-operation between the two partners don't correct the problem after a reasonable length of time, psychotherapy and sexual retraining under the direction of a specialist may be required.

Somehow another sexual difficulty has become associated with impotency, although they are not related. *Premature ejaculation* is considered to be so when it occurs before penetration or within a few seconds afterward. Since in our culture the ability to prolong intercourse has become a gauge of masculinity, many men think they're sexually inadequate partners if intercourse is, for them, a brief act, and they erroneously label as premature their hasty ejaculation. In one study, however, about 75 percent of the males reported that their ejaculations occurred within 2 minutes after penetration, and in many cases within 20 seconds. If such a high percentage of sexually capable men have this experience repeatedly, it is hard to understand why early ejaculation is thought of so often as a form of impotence. Fortunately, a man can learn to delay his ejaculation. Again, overcoming the problem requires the cooperation of his sex partner and perhaps sexual retraining under the supervision of a trained professional therapist. Since prolonged intercourse is more enjoyable and satisfying to both male and female, a man should not ignore the problem, even though it is so widespread.

Psychological factors often dominate physiological factors in sexual matters, and this is particularly evident in such disorders as *vaginismus,* an extremely powerful and often severely painful contraction of the muscles surrounding the vaginal tract. Anticipating the supposed pain of first sexual intercourse, or fear or guilt about intercourse can cause these muscular spasms, which may last for long periods of time. Even an attempt at penetration by the penis or the insertion of a finger into the vagina will often produce severe, agonizing pain. Males and females must understand the causes behind vaginismus, and avoid behavior that will produce discomfort in either partner. A selfish, inconsiderate or brutal husband can do permanent damage to a marriage, for example, if he pushes ahead like a battering ram in his attempts at intercourse when his wife is suffering these muscular spasms.

Oddly, this particular disorder occurs almost exclusively among women in the upper economic and educational groups. Sometimes local anesthetics applied to the vulva and vagina before penetration is attempted are successful in reducing the pain. A physician can also supply a young woman with instruments to stretch the vaginal muscles so that she can receive the penis comfortably. Since vaginismus has its roots so often in psychological problems involving fear, guilt and shame, psychotherapy and a sex training program are often called for to correct it.

A more common complaint, particularly among adolescents, is the discomfort from congested ovaries and congested testicles. The young have different names for them, like "lovers' nuts," and "stone ache." Girls may develop congested ovaries if they take part in prolonged, sexually stimulating petting which is not followed by release through orgasm. Prolonged but unrelieved sexual tensions cause blood to concentrate in the ovaries and other areas of the genitalia, producing a swelling and congestion of the tissues, which is the source of the pain.

In men, a long period of sexual excitement without relief causes a concentration of blood in the testicles, which creates conditions of swelling, pain, and aching. This condition is easily relieved in both girls and boys by masturbation to orgasm.

Nymphomania is a term applied long ago to women whose sex hunger is so strong that it overshadows all their other activities, and whose craving for sex is never satisfied no matter how many orgasms and other pleasures they get from it. So much popular mythology has been built up about this that Kinsey's definition, which I quoted at the beginning of the chapter, is particularly relevant today, when it would be difficult to find a clinician willing to classify this kind of sexuality as an authentic disorder.

It is not so much the "excessive" character of this behavior that makes it a category at all, since what is excessive is nearly impossible to establish, as it is its compulsive aspect, because it leads women to the typical unreasonable and self-defeating activities common to any kind of compulsion. Usually these women have an extreme need to be loved and accepted, a carryover of early childhood emphasis on the value of the body as a tool to gain attention, recognition and acceptance. There may also be fears of frigidity or latent homosexuality, against which the compulsive behavior is a defense. Again, such a woman may be using the opposite sex as an unconscious means of fulfilling a long-standing need for love from a substitute for a father who neglected her during childhood.

About the only successful method of treating this condition is to help the patient, through psychotherapy, to a better self-evaluation, to see herself as a worthwhile person who has something to offer the world other than her sexuality, and to see love as something besides sexual expression.

There is widespread misuse of the word "nymphomaniac," women being so labeled if they simply exhibit a strong desire for sex. Men, for instance, who don't understand the need of many sexually mature women for more than one orgasm during a single sexual experience, are likely to believe that they are involved with a sexual freak, an insatiable female. Then there are those ignorant, and sometimes cruel, men who accuse their wives of nymphomania simply because their wife's sexual desire exceeds their own.

If a man has feelings of inferiority and uncertainty about his own masculinity, he is likely to be so threatened by a woman who desires intercourse more frequently than he does that he must find some way to fight her. Consequently he calls her a "nymphomaniac" and "abnormal." By implication, he is the normal one.

The same condition in men is known as *satyriasis,* a word coined by the same early sexologist, Krafft-Ebing, who manufactured "nymphomania." In old books on the subject, a great deal of nonsense was written about the supposed physiological basis of both these conditions, but we know now that the causes are psychological and the same for men as for women, with the added factor in men that there may be an unconscious attempt to strengthen their view of themselves where masculinity and adequacy are concerned.

As one might expect, the public is not nearly as concerned about "oversexed" men as it is about "nymphomaniac" women; in fact, there is a whole category of women who think *all* men are oversexed. The difference in attitudes, of course, has its roots in the traditional sexual role assigned to women of being sexually passive. When they don't assume that role, their behavior becomes suspicious. In the instances when sexual activity is truly compulsive it can be treated successfully in both sexes with psychotherapy.

Promiscuity is another word that is hard to define. We regard it as participation in sexual intercourse with many people on a more or less casual basis. But what is "many"? At what point does variety become promiscuity? Maybe the word "casual" is a better key to understanding here. When sex becomes so casual that it really doesn't seem to make any difference who the partner is, we can legitimately say that the person is promiscuous. In men, this condition is accepted, or at least tolerated, by reason of the double standard, but in women it is strongly condemned.

When we study the personalities and family backgrounds of promiscuous women, it becomes clear that they are not, in general, evenly developed in their physical, emotional, intellectual and social maturity. Before they left home, these women participated very little in such group interaction as sports, and could not enter into organized group experiences, or accept the responsibility for their own behavior. Parents, husbands and friends were usually blamed for their failures and difficulties. Their promiscuity, then, was not caused by a strong sex drive, but, rather, sex was used in an attempt to solve other emotional problems.

In men, this condition is known as "Don Juanism," after the renowned lover, and it follows the same patterns of behavior. Studying them shows that almost all of their behavior stems from feelings of inadequacy, emotional conflicts, and other personality problems. Again, there is no evidence that their sex drive is stronger than anyone else's.

When sexual intercourse involves the exchange of money, it becomes *prostitution,* an institution so rooted in antiquity that it is known as "the oldest profession." Condemned and attacked by people in Western society, frequently the object of zealous people who think they can stamp it out, prostitution nevertheless continues to flourish in nearly every country and at all times. Legal efforts to abolish it have been flat failures. It has only been dealt with successfully, as in the Netherlands and West Germany, when it is licensed, controlled and segregated—and, even then, it tends to "slop over."

Prostitution presents problems beyond whatever questions of morality may be considered. Unless it is licensed and the girls examined, as they are in the two countries cited, it is a breeding ground for VD; in the United States, the VD rate is extremely high among prostitutes. It is also subject to exploitation both by organized crime and by the small-time racketeers called pimps, who control one or more women and act as both managers and lovers. Other criminal activity, particularly narcotics, often follows in the wake of this exploitation. Thus prostitution becomes a social problem in which the sexual behavior itself plays only a small part, although of course it is the key.

Unlike other countries, prostitution seems to be on the decline in the United States. In Kinsey's first study in 1948, he found that about 70 percent of white males had had some experience with prostitutes. More recent studies indicate a steady decrease in the number of professionals, and in the frequency with which men visit them, although there are so many imponderables involved here that it's difficult to be sure about this. Some authorities argue that the opposite has occurred. Those who say it is declining point out that going to a prostitute has traditionally been a learning experience about sex for boys and young men, and this has gradually been replaced by intercourse with their girl friends, in an era of greater sexual freedom. Certainly it would be better if that were true, since boys would get a far better idea of what sex was all about from a girl friend than from a prostitute. What might be gained from professionalism is lost in the shabby atmosphere, the fears that accompany it, the mechanical, emotionless character of the act, and the pressure the prostitute puts on the man to "hurry and finish" so she can go to the next customer. (This pressure is known to be one of the main causes of premature ejaculation.)

Prostitutes lead a hard life, in that they are exploited by their pimps, by corrupt policemen and by organized crime. They are in constant danger not only of jail, but of bad, even possibly fatal, treatment from their customers, who may be sadistic, deranged, or, at best, obsessed with needs for gratification which involve debasing them even further. Yet there is no real lack of recruits. Aside from the very few who are kidnapped or otherwise forced into prostitution, most of these girls, contrary to popular belief, get into it because they want to, and many of them enjoy it, in spite of everything. Those at the lower level usually have little intelligence and education. Some have come into "the life," as it is called, out of a desire for adventure, but far more do so in order to support a drug habit, or the habit of their pimp. Still others are highly sexed and enjoy the promiscuity of the life. There are those, too, who have a neurotic need to punish and degrade themselves, or their activities are an act of rebellion against parents and society. Most at this level are of such low-grade intelligence, so emotionally disturbed, or so lazy that they are unable to be regularly employed. Most of the prostitutes state that they are in the profession because it is an easy way to make money

On another level, as there have always been, are girls who get very high prices for their services, live in expensive apartments, and have their sex only with the executives and public officials who can afford them. These "call girls" sometimes marry one of their customers, or organize a small circle of other girls and run it as a business. In these girls, the emotional disturbance is likely to be more complicated, and the intelligence considerably higher.

Rape has come into new prominence lately because of the effort by both men and women to exert better controls over what they consider a particular outrage. Rape is sexual intercourse forced on an unwilling person, nearly always a woman. Legally, the difficulty has centered on the word "unwilling," which, because of our judicial system, is unreasonably difficult to prove.

Penalties for rape are severe, when convictions are obtained. In most states, maximum sentence is life imprisonment (it was death before the recent Supreme Court ruling invalidated the death penalty), but 15 to 20 years is a more usual sentence. The rape victim is statistically between 18 and 25 in most cases, although very young children or old women are not immune. The rapist is typically about 26, from a low-income, culturally deprived background. He is often mentally retarded, or of no more than dull-normal intelligence. He is likely to have emotionally unstable parents and a weak, often alcoholic, father. The majority come from broken homes. Rapists are usually emotionally immature. They had little supervision from their parents when they were young, and they are frequently unattractive physically. Rapists have criminal minds, usually, in the sense that they are accustomed to taking what they want when they want it, whether it is money, a car, or a woman. Rape, consequently, is most often just another aspect of overall criminal behavior.

One reason why rape convictions have been difficult to get is the fact that there are some emotionally disturbed women who accuse a man of rape even though no intercourse has taken place; he may even be a total stranger. Again, an adult woman who consents to the act sometimes charges the man with rape as an act of revenge, or because she projects her feelings of guilt, which her conscience cannot handle, onto the man, who participated in the sexual act no more freely than she did. Since these cases do occur, law enforcement officials have taken advantage of that fact in other cases where no such behavior is involved. Injustices occur in both instances.

As the law defines it, *statutory rape* is intercourse with a girl under the legal age of consent, usually 18. Even though many girls in these cases may have lied about their ages and purposely encouraged the accused man to have intercourse with them, the law presumes that because they are so young they are incapable of forming a mature judgment about the nature and possible result of their actions. One study disclosed that about a third of the men convicted on charges of rape were accused on statutory grounds. Although it is a rarity, it sometimes happens that a women is charged with raping a male, and in these cases it is almost always statutory rape because the boy involved is under age. A woman may also be accused and sentenced in rape cases when she has aided a man in raping another woman.

Things you thought you knew but didn't

B Y THIS TIME I'M SURE you're aware that misinformation and superstition surround human sexuality. I've tried to dispel some of these myths and fallacies along the way, but there are many that I haven't even mentioned. It's important to demolish as many as possible, I think, because so much of this misinformation has been passed from generation to generation, by parents, teachers, and even doctors, that the cycle will never be broken until enough people have facts instead of myths.

I should add that beliefs about sexual matters for which there is no foundation are not limited to uneducated and unsophisticated people. Highly educated professionals sometimes show that they, too, are the possessors of an incredible collection of sexual mythology, and the danger is that they will hand it down as being absolute truth to those whom they influence and teach.

Here are some of the most common myths and fallacies:

1. *That each individual is allotted just so many sexual experiences and when these are used up, sexual activity is finished for that person.*

This notion has plagued mankind for centuries, and it is totally false. In fact, quite the opposite is true. The earlier men or women mature physically, the longer their sexual reproductive ability continues; and the more sexually active a person is and the earlier he begins his activity, the longer it is likely to continue into old age. It isn't *necessarily* true, I hasten to say, that if a person starts his sex life early he will be guaranteed a longer and consistently vigorous sex life. I simply mean that ordinarily the person with a stronger sex drive than average will begin sexual activity earlier in life and will continue it longer.

Sometimes this particular myth takes the form of saying that men have only a certain amount of semen or a certain number of sperm cells in their bodies, and once the supply has been discharged, no more sperm or semen can be manufactured. Adults have used this argument in attempting to discourage boys from masturbating. A good many boys have grown up believing that each ejaculation takes from their body some amount of protein, blood, strength or what have you, and it will be difficult or impossible to replace. On the contrary, experts in how hormones function have shown that the chemical makeup of semen is constantly being replenished by a normal intake of food, and the production of sperm is also a continuing process. Consequently, ejaculated sperm are easily and quickly replaced in the healthy body, much the way saliva is constantly replenished.

It is virtually impossible physically for a person to experience orgasm or ejaculation too often. As I noted earlier, when you reach your physiological limit, the sex act becomes unpleasant, and for the man, it becomes impossible to perform. After a normal rest or recovery period, however, both the desire and ability to have sex return to normal.

2. *That an unborn child can be "marked."* You'll often hear someone say, when a pregnant woman has had a sudden shock or fright, "Poor woman! That means her child will be born with a birthmark." Since there is so close a connection between fetus and mother, it's easy to understand why people can believe that such experiences might cause a baby to be born with some physical or emotional mark. But there is no direct connection between either the nervous systems or the blood systems of mother and fetus, so the idea a child can be "marked" in this way is false.

It happens sometimes that a child *is* born with an unusual birthmark—for example, a skin discoloration in the shape of a bird—and then the parents may "remember" that while the mother was pregnant she was attacked or frightened by something with the general shape of the birthmark.

This is not to say, however, that the diet and chemical intake of the mother don't have a direct effect on certain physiological reactions of the child, both before and after birth, since she does supply nourishment for the fetus. If she greatly overeats certain foods, for example, it is possible that an allergic condition may develop in the child, continuing after birth. It is well known, too, that the physical condition of infants whose mothers smoke tobacco during their pregnancies will be affected by it. But these reactions have nothing to do with "marking" a baby, which is a physiological and psychological impossibility.

3. *That sexual intercourse should be avoided during pregnancy.* We know a good deal about the pregnant woman's physical and psychological responses to sexual stimulation. Numerous investigations have shown that, in general, there is little change in a woman's sexual interest and capacity for enjoyment during the first three months of her pregnancy, and, in fact, during the second three months there is usually an increase in erotic feelings, perhaps even greater than she experiences when she is not pregnant. It is not until the final three months that most women show a loss in sexual interest. There is no evidence to indicate that the pregnant woman with no unusual physical problems should not engage regularly in intercourse to orgasm until late in the third three-

month period. Naturally, sensible precautions should be taken against excessive pressure on the abdomen, deep penetration of the penis, and infection.

Only one thing needs to be remembered. During a woman's orgasmic response, there are rather strong contractions of the uterus, not unlike those experienced during labor, and they might cause labor contractions to begin if the woman is within six to three weeks of delivery. Otherwise, intercourse can be continued safely up to that time, as long as there is no pain during the act, if the fetal membrane is intact, and if there is no spotting or bleeding. Intercourse should actually be encouraged, if the woman wishes it. But whether or not intercourse takes place during the final period of pregnancy and the early period after it is an individual matter, to be decided by the woman and her doctor, who must make his decision on each individual case.

4. *That oral-genital sex between a man and woman indicates homosexual tendencies.* It's hard to understand how this one started. The determining factor in homosexuality is the choice of a partner of the same sex rather than the opposite one, not the technique that is used. Genuinely masculine men and very feminine women often enjoy oral-genital contact, but unless that kind of activity is preferred with a member of the *same* sex, it simply can't be an indication of homosexual tendencies. I suppose the idea may stem from the fact that homosexuals often use oral-genital techniques, but it doesn't follow that these are solely characteristic of homosexuals.

5. *That repeated sexual experiences with one man will leave a mark on a child later fathered by another man.* This theory has been talked about and written about enough so that it has a name—*telegony*. Some breeders of animals accept it. But there is no scientific basis for this theory, whether one is discussing humans or animals. Inadequate knowledge of the laws of heredity and unscientific methods of observation and control in animal breeding have led some people to the conclusion that, on the human level, the offspring of a second husband might bear some characteristics of the wife's first husband.

There are recorded cases where a white woman who had

previously borne children to a black man, and then later married a white man, subsequently bore children with what are loosely and no doubt inaccurately described as "Negro traits." But these children were either fathered by a man with "Negro traits," or the woman had some Negro blood in her own heritage. Any cause-and-effect relationship between her previous black husband and the Negroid features of children born to her marriage with a white man is a genetic impossibility.

Animal breeders who believe in telegony overlook the fact that female dogs remain in heat for several days, during which time they may mate with several males. Since they also have a way, unless watched closely, of escaping and mating with almost any or all of several male dogs that happen along, it is quite possible to find a litter of puppies in which not one resembles the intended sire. But this is not a carryover from the female dog's previous matings. It is simply that the puppies of the same litter have been sired by different dogs.

6. *That heart patients need not worry that sexual activity will be harmful to their health as long as they remain physically inactive and quiet during intercourse.*

Heart patients who don't understand the marked changes that always occur in heart rate and blood pressure during human sexual response may be endangering their lives or health by sexual arousal. During sexual excitement and fulfillment, the heart rate may increase from 70 beats per minute to 150 or more, and blood pressure may increase rapidly from 120 to 250 or more. Both husband and wife should understand that even if the heart patient plays a passive and physically inactive role during the sexual act, the heartbeat and blood pressure will still rise to very high peaks as a result of the sexual response alone.

It is quite possible for heart patients to lead an active sex life in some circumstances, and naturally there is considerable emotional benefit to be had from sensible sexual behavior. Heart patients may hear from a fellow victim that *his* doctor permits him to have intercourse as long as his wife lies on him or sits astride, and he takes a relatively passive role. But this is permissible in some conditions and not in others, so these patients need to follow their doctor's advice very carefully when it comes to sex, as well as in other aspects of their daily lives. If they have any doubt, they should consult another specialist.

7. *That the virginity of the woman is of great importance in the success of a marriage.*

No investigation of this subject has ever showed more than a slight relationship between happiness in marriage and premarital experience. The small relationship that does exist favors premarital chastity. It is true that women who are virgins when they marry tend to have longer marriages. But lengthy marriages are not necessarily happy ones; the couples merely stay together. We know, as I have discussed, that highly religious girls are more likely to be virginal when they marry than other girls are. Furthermore, highly religious girls tend to stay longer in a marriage—happy or otherwise—than do less religious girls. Thus, the lengthy marriages are in reality due to the religion factor and not the virginity, because when two groups of girls with the same religious involvement—one group virginal, one nonvirginal—are compared for longevity of marriage, no differences can be found.

Whether a woman has had premarital intercourse is not nearly as important to later marital adjustment as whether she has had an adequate sex education, enjoys emotional stability, is dependable, and possesses a measure of economic security. Since sexual adjustment in marriage is based on the couple's compatibility at many levels of day-to-day living together, having premarital intercourse, no matter how satisfactory it is, will not of itself assure a couple of a happy sex life after marriage. A girl should remember this when she hears a boy say that "no sensible person buys a pair of shoes without trying them on."

8. *That there is a difference between vaginal and clitoral orgasm.* This has been discussed to a degree in an earlier part of the book. You will remember that the question, which Kinsey was the first to study in any detailed way, is whether there is any such thing as a vaginal orgasm at all. In his opinion, there was not, and he had impressive data to support it. At the time, and later, Freudian psychoanalysts and a few other thera-

pists argued vehemently that the vaginal orgasm did exist be cause women told them it did, and, besides, it was an integral part of their psychoanalytic theory.

Freud and the school that followed his believed that only mature women had vaginal orgasms; those that were produced by manipulating the clitoris, they said, were signs of immaturity and sexual inadequacy. Not many therapists, particularly since the work of Masters and Johnson was published, believe this idea any more. It has been well established that the vaginal walls themselves contain few sex nerve endings, and that only stimulation, direct or indirect, of the clitoris and surrounding areas produces orgasmic response in the vast majority of women.

From a purely physiological viewpoint, direct clitoral stimulation usually produces a somewhat stronger orgasmic response than the indirect stimulation of the clitoris that occurs during vaginal penetration. Many women find the indirect stimulation of sexual intercourse more satisfying, however, because of the psychological factors involved—for one thing, the great closeness with the partner that it permits.

To talk about clitoral or vaginal orgasm is somewhat meaningless since the orgasmic response involves the entire body, both mental and physical. For example, some women can have orgasms by breast manipulation alone while others can achieve orgasm by fantasy alone. But there is no doubt that stimulation of the clitoris and vulva produces far more sexual arousal and response than vaginal stimulation does.

9. *That menopause or hysterectomy ends a woman's sex life.*

There is now abundant evidence that a woman's sexual desire usually continues with the same strength until she is 60, and very often much beyond that age. Because sexual desire does exist long after the menopausal changes in hormone functioning, this is a clear indication that ordinarily there are no physical reasons for a woman's sex life to end because of menopause or hysterectomy. It is easy to see why doctors thought so in the past. No doubt they reasoned that since the ovaries' production of female sex hormones decreases at the menopause and afterward, a woman's sex drive would also decrease. Modern research, however, indicates that hormones are only one of many factors affecting the capacity for sexual response. Besides, it is the androgen produced by her adrenal glands, not estrogen or progesterone produced by her ovaries, that affects a woman's sex drive. More important are such psychological factors as the woman's emotional stability and her attitude toward sex.

As for total hysterectomy, as I have noted in another chapter, this is a removal of the uterus, compared with what is called a panhysterectomy, meaning removal of uterus, Fallopian tubes and ovaries. In a total hysterectomy, there would not be a significant loss of hormonal balance to account for any loss of sex drive. If the doctor explains the effects of the operation, neither should there be any psychological reason for any lessening of the sex drive. If the ovaries and tubes are also removed, hormonal changes will occur, although medication can make up any losses. In brief, whether or not a woman has a hysterectomy, and in spite of menopause, she can expect to maintain her sex drive at approximately the same level between the ages of 30 and 60, with only a gradual diminishing afterward.

10. *That blacks have greater sex drive than whites, and that the black male's penis is larger than the white male's.*

This is one of the odder racist notions. In fact, there is no scientific evidence to support the belief that one race is more sexually active than another. Some researchers have found a greater amount of sexual activity among poorly educated Americans of low socio-economic status than among those more fortunate. Since the number of blacks in this category is greater than the number of whites, people have concluded erroneously that racial rather than environmental or class factors account for the differences in sexual activity. A recent Duke University investigation into sexual behavior during the aging process demonstrated that black subjects between the ages of 60 and 93 were more active sexually than whites in that age bracket, but these researchers also pointed out that more of the black subjects were of the lower socio-economic classes than the whites.

Another myth of the same kind is the mistaken teaching

that culturally and economically deprived people are more primitive and aggressive, and so presumably more sexually potent, than people from higher levels. This prejudicial belief leads many people to exaggerate the sexual powers of black people.

A great many whites firmly but erroneously believe that a black man's penis is larger than the white man's, and that the larger the penis, the greater a man's sexual powers, black or white. But it has been established for some time that the size of the penis has absolutely nothing to do with the sexual ability of a man, except in those cases where hormonal deficiency has stunted both the growth of the penis and the sexual drive. The idea that the black man's limp penis is somewhat larger than the white man's probably stems from the fact that black and white male body structures are somewhat different (the black man has longer legs but a smaller chest cavity, accounting, for example, for the superiority of the black sprinter and of the white distance runner). But even if this were true, there is little or no relationship between the largeness or smallness of the penis when it is limp and when it is erect.

11. *That a large penis is important to a woman's sexual gratification and that the man with a large penis is more sexually potent than the man with a small one.*

Again, the myth of penis size, and again—there is virtually no relationship between size and a man's ability to satisfy a woman sexually. There are four possible exceptions: When a woman *thinks* penis size makes a difference, creating a psychological difficulty; when sexual pleasure is decreased because the penis is too large and causes the woman pain; when the penis is so abnormally small that penetration and pelvic contact cannot be maintained; or when a woman's vagina becomes quite loose following the birth of several children.

Not only is there little relationship between body size and penis size, but there is far less relationship than between the dimensions of other organs and body size. The size of the penis is determined by heredity, and in no way affects sexual potency, favorably or unfavorably. Probably the myths surrounding the large penis had their beginnings in the younger boy's awed view of the older boy's larger penis, and by the older one's frequent braggings about his great sexual feats, which are usually wishful thinking. It is easy to see how younger boys came to associate larger genitals with extraordinary sexual ability, and how this myth was perpetuated.

12. *That today's young adults are "going wild" sexually.*

Older generations, since ancient Greece and before, have believed this about younger ones. Socrates was complaining 2500 years ago that the young had contempt for authority, showed disrespect for their elders, and would rather talk than exercise. "Children are now tyrants, not the servants of their households," he grumbled.

There was never, at any time, the slightest proof that today's young people are a lesser breed than generations past. Today's youth, in fact, are more aware of social injustice, of environmental problems, and of morality than many of the older generation are. Sexually, very few changes are occurring in the behavior of boys and girls today, although they have evolved new standards of thinking, believing and behaving, as every generation has done.

13. *That frigid women, promiscuous women, and prostitutes are not so likely to become pregnant as women whose sexual activity is more normal.*

Since frigidity in women is practically always based on psychological factors, and since conception has nothing whatever to do with whether or not a woman enjoys sexual activity, it is obvious that there is no foundation to the first part of this myth. If a woman attempts to prevent conception by holding herself back from orgasm, or by remaining passive and indifferent during intercourse, she is running just as much risk of pregnancy as the one who is unrestrained. Neither orgasm nor active participation is necessary to conception. If promiscuous women and prostitutes don't appear to become pregnant as readily, it's because they take better precautions. A pregnant prostitute is putting herself out of business; naturally, she takes extra precautions.

Some prostitutes, it is true, are sterile because of present or past venereal infection. But frequent intercourse in itself doesn't lessen the chance of a woman's becoming pregnant, nor does it increase the possibility of becoming sterile. Men, however, can lessen their ability to impregnate by frequent ejaculations because their sperm count is reduced. The average man requires 30 to 40 hours to regain his normal sperm count after ejaculation.

14. *That it is dangerous to have sexual intercourse during menstruation.*

This and other myths about menstruation have been with us for centuries. As early as 60 A. D., Pliny was telling his fellow Romans that the mere presence of a menstruating woman would cause "new wine to become sour, seeds to become sterile, fruit to fall from trees, and garden plants to become parched." Menstrual fluid, this otherwise able historian went on, could blunt the edge of steel, kill a swarm of bees, rust iron and brass instantly, and if by chance dogs were to taste it, they would become mad and their bite would be venomous and incurable.

With this kind of foundation, it is no wonder that couples shied away from intercourse during menstruation. The taboo against "wasting sperm" by having intercourse during the "safe period" of menstruation undoubtedly added to the cluster of misinformation surrounding intercourse.

The fact is that menstrual blood is perfectly harmless to both men and women. The source of the flow is the uterus, not the vagina, and no tissue damage occurs from the penis's penetration. A woman's sex drive ordinarily does not decrease during her period; in fact, it may increase.

A related myth about menstruation is that women should not bathe during the time of the flow. It is true that sharp changes in temperature during bathing may temporarily stop the bleeding, and so a woman should take precautions against any such abrupt change. But otherwise there is no reason why bathing, or any other normal everyday activity such as dancing, tennis, bowling, etc., cannot be carried on.

15. *That humans can get "hung up," that is, be unable to withdraw, during intercourse.*

This idea results from man's observation of animals and trying to relate their behavior to his own. Dogs do get "hung up" because of the peculiar structure of the male dog's sex organs. There is a bone in the animal's penis that enables him to penetrate the bitch's vagina before full erection. When that is attained, the head of the penis fills the vaginal barrel, and at the same time the walls of the female dog's vagina swell. All of this serves to "trap" the penis and prevent its withdrawal before ejaculation.

One of the most common of those stories that are always told as true, and that have spread around the world, is about the couple who become locked together during intercourse, and a doctor is required before the penis can be released. There are a hundred variations of the story, at least. It always seems to have happened to a friend, or a friend of a friend.

Theoretically, of course, it is possible for a woman to experience the sudden strong muscle spasms of the vagina I described earlier, called *vaginismus,* during sexual intercourse, and the vagina may momentarily tighten around her partner's penis. But even in those circumstances, the pain or fear that the man would experience is enough to cause loss of erection, permitting easy withdrawal. There is not a single verified case of "hang up" among humans.

16. *That nature makes up for the number of males killed during time of war.*

Man depends on the laws of nature to keep his life in balance, and after a war, he finds some comfort in the notion that nature makes up for the killing by increasing, in some mystical way, the ratio of male to female births. This idea was reinforced by the fact that after both World Wars there was, in fact, an increase in male births, but scientists have determined that there were other reasons for this phenomenon.

At any time, many more males than females are conceived, but from the time of conception on, the female survival rate is higher than the male's. The conception ratio is about 160 males to 100 females. The ratio of fertilized egg implantation into the uterine wall is about 120 males to 100 females, and the birth ratio is 105 males to 100 females. If it appears that more males are born after a war, that is probably because people marry at a younger age. The younger mothers are strong and healthy, giving fertilized ova a greater chance for survival and implantation, thus tending to give birth to a higher percentage of males than older mothers do. Since these mothers are separated from their husbands, the enforced spacing between births is longer than usual, leaving the wives in a stronger physical condition to carry the next child to term, thus increasing the likelihood of a male birth. In brief, since among younger women more male zygotes are implanted in the uterus and fewer male embryos die, there is a greater male-to-female ratio of births.

17. *That circumcision makes it difficult for a man to control ejaculation, or that the lack of circumcision makes control of ejaculation difficult.*

Until recently, the first of these fallacies was frequently accepted as a biologic fact. It was assumed that the glans of the circumcised penis is more sensitive than the uncircumcised penis to the frictions of masturbation or intercourse; consequently the circumcised man could not delay ejaculation as long as the man whose foreskin was still intact. Research, however, has failed to discover any differences in the sensitivity of a circumcised penis and one that isn't. In most cases, the foreskin retracts from over the glans of the uncircumcised penis during a state of erection, especially during intercourse, permitting the same exposure of the glans that the circumcised glans gets during the sex act. But even in the cases where it doesn't fully retract, the response to stimulation of the uncircumcised penis is the same.

The second of these fallacies rises from the notion that circumcision unduly exposes the glans of the penis at all times, toughening its tissue to an unusual degree and making it less sensitive to stimulation, thereby causing the ejaculatory processes to be slowed down. Medical evidence does not support this contention.

18. *That urination by the woman after intercourse, or having intercourse while standing, will prevent pregnancy.*

Since the bladder does not empty through the vagina, urine cannot possibly wash out sperm deposited in the vaginal canal during intercourse. There is a remote possibility that if the woman urinates immediately after intercourse, the position assumed for that act might aid in preventing the sperm from entering the uterus. But urination itself has no effect.

As for the other myth, pregnancy can be produced no

matter what the position chosen for intercourse—lying, standing, sitting, or any other position. Sperm are deposited at or
near the cervix upon ejaculation and almost immediately
afterward they begin to move forward and into the uterus.
The standing position is not likely to cause the sperm to spill
out of the vagina before they can enter the uterus and make
their way toward the ovum, if one is present in the uterine
tubes.

19. *That humans and animals below the human level can
crossbreed.*

This myth was fostered for years in the Sunday supplements
by wild tales of scientific parties embarking for deepest, dark-
est Asia, taking a woman with them to mate with a gorilla or
some other anthropoid, with the intention of producing the
"missing link." But alas for the wishful thinking of the busy
feature writers, not only is it impossible for humans to crossbreed with animals below the human level, but interbreeding
among various kinds of lower animals is equally impossible,
although members of different species of the same type may
produce crossbred offspring, like the tigron, the offspring of
a tigress and a lion. But a man and an ape cannot interbreed,
nor can an ape and a tiger. Tigers and lions are both members
of the cat family.

20. *That simultaneous climaxes are necessary if conception
is to take place.*

To prove the falseness of this belief, it is only necessary to
point out that a woman can be made pregnant through artificial insemination, without any orgasm at all when it is done.
The presence or absence of orgasmic response has nothing to
do with whether or not a woman becomes pregnant. If she
produces a mature, healthy egg that is penetrated by a normal
sperm, conception takes place.

21. *That athletes should abstain from any sexual activity for
several days before participating in athletic events such as
football or track.*

This ancient myth was even being debated (and taken seriously) as late as the 1972 Olympic Games. There is not the
slightest evidence to show that sexual functioning is in any
way harmful. Neither is an athlete's strength permanently or

even temporarily depleted by intercourse or any other kind of sexual activity. On the contrary, enforced abstinence from sexual activity over a long period of time often causes undue tension in athletes, especially married ones who are on long tours away from their wives. In fact, Kinsey reports a track athlete who broke a world record immediately after masturbating to relieve tension.

The production of sperm is a constant and steady process, and no more sperm are produced or "depleted" from the body if people have frequent sexual activity than if they don't. Probably this popular misconception comes from the noticeable relaxation a man experiences immediately after orgasm, and it is confused with fatigue, which might interfere with high-level athletic performance. They are not the same thing.

22. *That girls from the South, or from tropical regions, mature sexually at an earlier age than girls from the North or more temperate climates.*

This popular belief has been challenged recently. Studies have shown that girls from tropical Nigeria begin menstruating on the average at 14.2 years, while in temperate England it is 13.7, an inconsiderable difference. The time is almost identical in India, Yugoslavia and Denmark, which cover a wide range of climates. Similar findings have been made when American girls from the Southern and Northern regions of the country have been compared.

23. *That through the use of certain foods, drugs, or mechanical devices, known collectively as aphrodisiacs, people can increase their sexual desire and abilities.*

Since the beginning of civilization, man has attempted to stimulate his sex drive, frequently through exotic new foods. High hopes, for example, were held out for the potato, when it was first brought to England. Others put their trust in food with a superficial physical similarity to a sex organ, like the oyster or the banana.

Alcohol is probably the most famous of the alleged sexual stimulants—Ogden Nash wrote, "Candy is dandy/But liquor is quicker"—but in reality it is a depressant which interferes with the normal functioning of the brain, slows body reflexes, and so decreases sexual abilities. If alcohol appears to heighten sexual desires in some instances, it is because it tends to remove, temporarily, feelings of guilt and fear from the minds of some people, making them less inhibited than they normally would be.

Among the so-called aphrodisiac drugs, the best known is "Spanish fly," obtained from a beetle. It does little more, however, than to cause acute irritation of the genital and urinary tracts. This drug can produce erection of the penis because of the dilation of local blood vessels, but the erection is not accompanied by any increase in sexual desire. Moreover, Spanish fly is a dangerous drug. Taken in excess, which varies with individuals, it can even cause violent illness or death.

Among the mechanical devices which have lately blossomed in sex shops both in America and Europe, the most common, besides the artificial penises and vaginas, which are not strictly aphrodisiacs, seem to be those rubber devices with uneven edges, or adorned with feathers, which are sometimes called "French ticklers." They don't tickle any more than the human hand, and in some circumstances, they can be harmful to the delicate membrane of the vaginal lining.

Marijuana has acquired the reputation of being an aphrodisiac, a fact which frightens the adult population and intrigues the younger generation. One of the reasons why adults are so fearful of marijuana is that they believe it to lead to sexual promiscuity. The truth is that marijuana is just as likely to "turn off" a sexually inexperienced young person as it is to cause him to "turn on." Couples who have a long standing sexual relationship find that marijuana enhances their sexual enjoyment because it distorts their time perception, making orgasm seem to last much longer than it actually does. Like alcohol, marijuana, LSD, and other drugs may reduce inhibitions and make a person more receptive to suggestion and erotic stimuli than he would be otherwise, but they are not true aphrodisiacs.

In short, there is no such thing as an aphrodisiac. In spite of a great many extravagant claims, some serious and others not, there is no kind of food or drug available on the market today which increases sexual desire or potency, and no mechanical device which does it either. Any good effects an aphrodisiac may have are entirely psychological, and these are likely to be temporary. The best aphrodisiacs are good health, plenty of rest and sleep, an adequate amount of exercise, and freedom from emotional tension.

24. *That through the use of certain drugs or devices, known collectively as anaphrodisiacs, people can decrease their sexual desire and ability.*

Perverse creature that he is, man has also for centuries tried to decrease sexual interest through such varied techniques as cold baths, the wearing of chastity belts and penis cages, and the use of chemicals. Best known of the chemicals is potassium nitrate, or saltpeter, widely used for years in prisons and school dormitories in the belief that it inhibited sexual desire. Actually, it is an almost completely neutral chemical and a complete failure as an anaphrodisiac. Other drugs used for this purpose can have unfortunate side effects.

If there is some valid reason, like an illness, why sexual activity should be reduced, any method of reduction should be part of an overall treatment by the physician. This situation is rare, however, because in illness, the individual's sexual interest and drive naturally decrease (with exceptions, like tuberculosis) according to the severity of the illness, and no control is necessary.

25. *That a seven-month fetus has a better chance to survive than an eight-month fetus.*

Another old wives' tale, often heard. It stems from the fact that most babies said to be seven-month infants are really nine-month. These "seven-month infants" are usually first-borns; it takes a girl about two months to find out that she is pregnant, and to make all the arrangements for the wedding. Dear Abby summed up this problem very well when she wrote, "The baby wasn't early, the marriage was late."

The older the fetus is at birth, the better its chance for survival, except in those instances when gestation has lasted too long and the placenta has begun to shrink.

There are so many other myths and fallacies about human sexuality that it would take pages more to list them. As a matter of fact I have written an entire book, *Sexual Myths and*

*Fallacies,** on this topic. The parent or student who is interested in pursuing this further is directed to this book. As you will remember, I've talked about some of these myths in earlier chapters. Here are a few more, all completely untrue:

That a child conceived while his parents are drunk will be born either mentally or physically defective, or will be alcoholic when grown.

That it is the woman who determines the sex of the child.

That intercourse must take place twice in the same period of time in order to conceive twins, three times for triplets, and so on.

That the diet of a woman during pregnancy will help determine the sex of the child.

That the fetus sleeps during the day and awakens (and kicks) during the night.

That male children are produced by ova from one ovary and females from the other, or that sperm from one testicle produce males and vice versa.

That the size of a man's penis can be judged by his foot size, and that the size of a woman's vagina can be judged by the size of her mouth.

That the uterus "sucks up" seminal fluid.

That women ejaculate, like men.

That lower animals menstruate.

That men who are bald have greater sexual drive and capacity than men with full heads of hair.

That the age at which a man is most likely to molest children is 65 or after.

That sex criminals are driven to their behavior by narcotics or pornography.

That sex offenders are typically antireligious.

That chronic sex offenders are oversexed.

That sex offenders cannot be cured.

That typical sex offenders, especially those who molest children, are aggressive, sadistic, homicidal and physically dangerous.

Sexual Myths and Fallacies is also published by Van Nostrand Reinhold Co., 450 West 33rd St., New York, N.Y. 10001.

That a child conceived in a rear-entry position of intercourse will be homosexual.

That men who enjoy having their nipples stimulated have hidden homosexual desires.

That most prostitutes are lesbians.

That the typical career woman has hidden lesbian tendencies.

That any lesbian will prefer a man if a "real man" just uses the right technique.

That women cannot have multiple orgasms.

That premature ejaculation is caused by an abnormally sensitive penis.

That wet dreams are indicators of sexual disorders.

That women do not have nocturnal orgasms.

That the best health is enjoyed by those who abstain from sex.

That men with superior physical development and strength, like football players, have a stronger sex drive and capability than frail and less athletically inclined men.

That if a woman wears high heels during pregnancy her baby will be cross-eyed or have some other physical problem.

That unusual or excessive sexual practices can cause mental breakdowns.

That the absence of the hymen (maidenhead) proves that a girl is not a virgin.

That taking the Pill will delay a woman's menopause.

That people suffering from sexual inadequacy can expect very little help from treatment for their problems.

That pornography has a corruptive effect on the minds and behavior of people, especially children.

That pornography stimulates people to commit criminal sex acts.

No doubt there are at least a hundred more. Ignorance never takes a holiday.

12

Sex
and the law

ONE OF THE WORST FAILURES OF the criminal justice system in the United States is the network of laws which purport to govern people's sexual behavior. Most of these laws were written more than a hundred years ago, many longer than that. Generally, they reflect the ignorance of the lawmakers on sexual matters, and most are unenforceable. Taken together, they are a jungle of vagueness, inconsistency, unreason and injustice. They are in conflict with each other, not only among the states but often within the same state, and anyone who studies them cannot help but feel the crying need for uniform Federal statutes, written on the basis of the latest scientific knowl-

191

edge instead of the prejudices, bigotries and general misinformation of the legislators.

In the past half-century, while society itself has been changing with bewildering speed, there have been few attempts to change the laws governing sex. Not long ago, a man in North Carolina was convicted and sentenced to 30 years in prison for homosexuality, an offense which the court called "the abominable and detestable crime against nature, not to be mentioned among Christians." A United States district judge who took the appeal in this case remarked drily that it might be a good idea if the North Carolina legislature overhauled that particular law. It was first passed in England in 1533! Not long after the North Carolina incident occurred, a self-admitted New York City homosexual announced his intention to run for civic office, and it created scarcely a ripple, as far as his sexual preference was concerned.

It is difficult to change sex laws beause of the fears and anxieties prevalent in the general population wherever anything sexual is concerned. Lawmakers have a built-in fear of doing anything that might cause voters to view their attitudes on sex, punishment, or morality as being too liberal.

Enforcement and administration of the laws we have relating to sex are extremely inconsistent. Very few sex law violators are actually prosecuted. There are, for example, an estimated three million homosexual acts performed in America for every conviction. Yet until recently, and even now in only a few states, lawmakers have consistently refused to consider even a slight relaxation and reworking of these laws, in spite of pleas from psychologists, psychiatrists, criminologists, sexologists, sociologists, and even many members of the clergy, as well as private citizens.

Until the Supreme Court recently ended the gross injustice, laws against abortion were especially outdated and unfair. It amounted to making abortion possible only for women who could afford to pay. We can be sure that even the Supreme Court decision will not end the struggle for justice in this particular area; the antiabortionists will be working night and day to find ways of evading it.

Many of our sex laws are simply contrary to reality. In certain states, for example, a married couple can be arrested and convicted, at least theoretically, for any sexual behavior that involves more than the insertion of the penis into the vagina, even though the act is carried out in the privacy of their bedroom. And according to the fuzzy laws of most states, 95 percent of adult American males and a large percentage of American women have had orgasms in an illegal manner.

In June 1967, the Supreme Court declared that laws banning marriages between members of different races were unconstitutional, yet such laws still remain in the legal codes of at least 16 states. Although the Court has recently ruled that the dissemination of birth control information to married couples is legal, the sale and use of birth control devices are still frowned on in some states.

The laws concerning obscenity and pornography are confusing, unrealistic, and subject to the manner in which particular courts, local, state or Federal (including the Supreme Court), define and interpret what is "obscene" or "pornographic" at any particular time. When President Nixon's Commission on Pornography and Obscenity, composed of distinguished Americans, attempted to bring some order out of this confusion in its report, the President rejected it. Basically, the trouble appears to be that most Americans regard sexual behavior with such strong emotion (shame, guilt and fear) that almost any written material or pictures that are of a sexual nature are likely to be interpreted by *someone* as being obscene, and therefore unlawful. Even *Alice in Wonderland, Huckleberry Finn, Robinson Crusoe* and other children's classics have been censored as obscene in recent times. One authority has observed that if the Bible had been written today, we would be lucky to get an expurgated edition, if in fact it could be published and distributed at all. Considering much of the hard core pornography that can be found in almost any bookstore, this authority is clearly behind the times.

If the laws themselves are hopelessly inconsistent, their enforcement is even more so, because of the beliefs and social attitudes of the judges and law enforcement officers. No better proof of this incredible muddle can be found than in the great variations in sentences handed out for the same offense by different courts. The makers and enforcers of the laws, of course, only reflect the inconsistencies in the attitudes of the general public toward sex and sex crimes. From time to time, the public demands even stricter laws in this area, citing the "increase" in sex crimes, but scientific study shows that there has been no great increase in sex crimes in recent years, in spite of the increase in public concern and the number of arrests. Those who have studied the problem say that the most realistic approach to sex offenders should be along the lines of understanding and treatment rather than punishment.

In the United States, about 40,000 arrests are made annually for major sexual offenses. In the state of New Jersey, which is not untypical, they break down this way: exhibitionists, 18 percent; rapists, 45 percent; "perverts," 14 percent; those involved in commercial sex, 7 percent; unclassified offenses, 16 percent.

Sex offenders are rarely involved in nonsexual crimes. They seem fairly well fixed on their particular form of sexual expression. Very few convicted sex offenders are the "sex fiends" of popular fiction. Most are rather harmless people who become involved in minor offenses. Only a small percentage, about 20 percent, use force or threats against their victims, and murder seldom occurs in connection with sexual offenses. In fact, the chances of being murdered by a "sex fiend" are considerably less than being done in by a relative or close friend; nine out of ten cases of murder occur within a family group or a close circle of friends. When murder occurs in sex crimes, the offender is usually mentally ill as well as sexually abnormal.

Arrested sexual offenders are usually found to be suffering from personality disturbances. In a study of 300 typical sex offenders, only 14 percent were psychologically "normal"; 29 percent were classified as mildly neurotic, 35 percent as severely neurotic, 8 percent as borderline psychotic, 5 percent as organically brain-damaged, 4 percent as mentally deficient, 3 percent as psychopathic, and 2 percent as psychotic.

The majority of arrested sex offenders come from low socio-economic backgrounds. They are poorly educated, and fall well below the average in intellectual capacity. Subnormal intelligence is more typical of offenders convicted of statutory rape, bestiality, incestuous relations, and sexually aggressive acts against little girls than of those convicted of forcible rape, exhibition, homosexuality and the distribution of "obscene" material.

Few sex criminals take narcotics or are under the influence of drugs when they commit their offense, but a large number of them, 32 percent, are under the influence of alcohol, especially when the offense involves sexual assault or incestuous relations with children.

Studies have disclosed that many imprisoned sex offenders have strong religious beliefs, and only a small percentage, 10 percent, claim to have been given no religious training in childhood. They read the Bible regularly, and faithfully go through the motions of practicing whatever faith they follow. They see themselves as devoted to their religion. Kinsey's investigations found the incest offender to be especially moralistic and religiously devout.

Exactly contrary to popular belief, the typical convicted sex offender is undersexed rather than oversexed, and is likely to be afraid of sexual contact with an adult female. He is severely inhibited sexually, except when the crime is statutory rape or incestuous acts against minors. The less emotionally disturbed the sex offender is, the less sexually restrained he tends to be.

Although the age of convicted sex offenders varies according to the specific kind of act committed, the majority are rather young, in their late teens or early twenties, and between 50 and 60 percent are unmarried. Most of them are the "losers" of society, so bungling and severely disturbed emotionally in all their behavior that their sexual offenses are likely to be carried out so stupidly it becomes easy to catch them. Intelligent sex offenders are not so likely to be discovered, and if arrested, are not so likely to be convicted.

Since his problem is primarily emotional, there is a real danger that the sex offender will repeat his offense unless he gets psychotherapy to help him understand and control his problems. Still, the rate of repetition, called recidivism, among convicted sex offenders is lower than that of other criminals. In a recent 13-year period, less than 10 percent of 4000 convicted sex offenders in one state institution became known repeaters. Public attention, unfortunately, centers on the 10 percent who repeat rather than the 90 percent who do not, and so parole boards are persuaded against the evidence of the statistics that all sex offenders are poor risks.

There is a tendency to lump all sex offenders under the name of "sexual psychopath," a term many psychologists and psychiatrists reject in this kind of general application. They point out that true sexual psychopaths constitute only 3 percent of all convicted sex offenders. Such offenders may use force or serious threat and are unable to control their sexual impulses. They form no close emotional attachments, show a lack of anxiety and remorse over their behavior, and may be troublemakers. They are not psychotic or feebleminded; in fact, they may give the appearance of being perfectly normal in every respect. A sexual psychopath, then, is a far cry from the typical convicted sex offender.

When we examine sex offenders as a group, they appear to fall into two broad classes, generally speaking. One group is involved in more or less normal behavior that is not very far from that of the general population, and is not believed to be brought about by unusual desires. Such acts do little or no psychological damage to the people involved, and have no lasting harmful effects on society, which nevertheless considers this conduct inappropriate and punishable. The man who occasionally becomes a "peeping Tom" is a good example. Considering the nature of such offenses, it is unrealistic to pass severe sentences or spend much time or money on these cases. More sensibly, effort ought to be directed toward helping these people make a better adjustment.

The second class of offenders is uncommon, and their truly unacceptable behavior is brought about by abnormal factors in their personalities. Their offenses may be a public nuisance, or be socially disorganizing, and may cause psychological or physical damage to those involved. Time and money would be well spent here, not only for detection but for research and treatment of their condition.

Sex laws ought to be designed to protect the individual from violence, to protect the young against adults who would take advantage of them, to protect the public from open display of sexual acts that might offend them, and to protect the family and marriage. These laws should *not* be written to determine and enforce rules of morality.

The statement above didn't come from me originally, but from principles set forth recently by the Illinois and Chicago Bar Associations in a proposed legal code to govern sexual behavior. The code, they declared, would adequately and realistically meet the needs of a modern society. These two groups of lawyers did what so many others had failed to do: they drew up and had accepted by the state legislature what is probably the most sensible and enforceable set of sex laws ever devised in this country.

Under the new Illinois laws, the legal definition of rape no longer includes "statutory" or "nonviolent" rape. A sexual act is not rape unless the male uses force against the female. If she gives her consent but is not of legal age, the offense is handled under a section of the law dealing with "contributing to the sexual delinquency of a child."

It is not illegal under the new code to engage in bestiality, nor are acts involving the sex organs of one person and the mouth or anus of another punishable, unless they are brought about by force, threat, or violence, or unless one partner is underage, or if the act is carried out so openly that it offends public decency. Such acts, whether heterosexual or homosexual, are not punishable if they are carried out by consenting adults and if conducted in private.

Punishment for incest in Illinois now takes into consideration the closeness of the relationship between the parties and their ages. Acts of incest which get the most severe penalties include father-daughter (no matter what her age), father-stepdaughter, and father-foster daughter—in the latter two cases, however, only if the girls are under 18. The strictness of this law is based on the fact that the father often holds a strong position in the family, and can have great influence over the daughters and their behavior.

"Public indecency" or "public exposure" is related to the place in which the act is carried out. A public place is described as "any place where the conduct may reasonably be expected to be viewed by others." In practice, this means that while a boy and a girl may be permitted to engage in light petting on a park bench, two men could not expect to get by with similar activity. However, a man would not be punished for suggesting to another man that they engage in such acts in private.

Illinois law now punishes men and women alike for prostitution, seeking customers for a prostitute, operating a place for prostitution, and visiting a prostitute. The law defines prostitution as accepting money for sexual intercourse or unusual sexual conduct, but it does not define as prostitution the acceptance of gifts other than money, such as jewelry, for sexual favors. This particular part of the state code attempts at least to bring some equality into laws against prostitution, although there is no evidence that this particular section will make any more sense than the others as far as controlling or eliminating prostitution is concerned.

The President's Crime Commission in May 1967 recommended that much sexual behavior now classified as criminal acts be removed from the law books. The commission argued that these acts are often social ills and not criminal matters, and should be treated that way. Fortunately, other states besides Illinois are beginning to recognize at last the need for a similar reworking of legal codes governing sexual activity.

At the Fourth International Convention on Criminology, held in 1960 at The Hague, Holland, attended by more than 600 government representatives and criminal law professors from almost every nation in the world, many recommendations to correct injustices in sex laws, and misuse of them, were adopted. They included recommendations calling for removal of fornication—that is, premarital intercourse—and adultery from the list of criminal offenses; the relaxing of interpretations of incest and reduction of the punishment for it; liberalization of the laws concerning birth control, abortion and artificial insemination; the granting of equal rights and freedom to homosexuals; and toughening of the laws concerning nonsupport of wives and children. If these recommendations were adopted, both individuals and society would certainly be greatly benefited.

Experts in law, psychology and sociology, or at least a great many of them, believe that laws governing sex should be limited to acts involving the use of force or threat, those that involve minors, and those that are performed in public. One of these experts, Albert Ellis, who has studied the psychology of sex offenders, has some other sensible recommendations to make:

1. Laws relating to sexual behavior should be rewritten in clear and exact terms.

2. A complete psychological examination should be performed on all persons accused of sex crimes in order to determine if they are sexually or psychologically abnormal, or if they are psychopaths who are unable to show necessary concern for others.

3. Psychological treatment should be provided for the sex offender in his own community while he is on probation, or if the offender is confined, it should be in an institution in which proper treatment is available. The offender should be kept carefully in protective custody as long as he is considered by authorities to be a threat to society.

4. Sex offenders should be offered help and understanding, rather than being punished and treated with scorn.

5. If prevention of sexual offenses is to be effective, accurate sex information must be made readily available to everyone, especially during the early years of childhood.

When a society refuses to improve the conditions of its sick and downtrodden, and when excessively severe punishment is handed down to offenders, something is certainly very wrong. People who treat the unfortunate that way are more likely to be motivated by hostilities and conflicts than any unselfish desire to protect the community.

In the end, a sense of social responsibility on the part of the public is going to be necessary to bring about needed changes in our sex laws. This means that the public must not only determine what is, or is not, a sex offense, but must also work toward a better understanding of the emotional makeup of the true sex offender, and of the part that guilt and conflict play in his sexual problems. Guilt about sexual matters begins early in childhood, when the child first starts exploring his sexual organs and is reprimanded or punished for it. It continues when any questions about sex are avoided or hushed up by the parents. Consequently, the growing child's sexual acts and desires are associated with feelings of guilt, and his ability to respond normally and naturally to his sexual drive is greatly impaired. Out of this guilt comes an almost endless number of psychological and sexual disturbances. An inability to perform sexually or disguised methods of expressing sexuality are only two of the results of poor sexual training.

All of us who work in this field hope that in time there will be a better understanding of human sexuality, and a consequent decrease in the number and severity of sexual problems. Only with such knowledge can society ever hope to work out effective methods of prevention or treatment of sexual conflicts and abnormalities.

The beginning of understanding is in sex education, but education is only the beginning. Whether it is effective rests with those who are being educated—you, the teenager. Only through your concern, your tolerance and understanding of human behavior, can an atmosphere be created in society in which all people can work out their own destinies, including their sexual destinies, in freedom from fear and ignorance.

INDEX